ENGLISH FURNITURE

SHIRE PUBLICATIONS

ENGLISH FURNITURE

JOHN BLY

Consultant Editor: Eric Knowles

SHIRE PUBLICATIONS

Published in Great Britain in 2010 by Shire Publications Ltd,
Midland House, West Way, Botley, Oxford OX2 0PH, United Kingdom.
44-02 23rd Street, Suite 219, Long Island City, New York 11101, USA.

E-mail: shire@shirebooks.co.uk · www.shirebooks.co.uk

© 2010 John Bly; Consultant Editor Eric Knowles.
This book is based on *Discovering English Furniture* by John Bly, first published in 1971.

A CIP catalogue record for this book is available from the British Library.

Shire Collections no. 5   ·   ISBN-13: 978 0 74780 786 5

John Bly has asserted his right under the Copyright, Designs and Patents Act, 1988, to be identified as the author of this book.

Designed by Ken Vail Graphic Design, Cambridge, UK and typeset in Bembo.
Printed in China through Worldprint Ltd.

10 11 12 13 14   10 9 8 7 6 5 4 3 2 1

FRONT COVER IMAGE
A pierced and carved mahogany chairback, exemplifying the solid but exuberant nature of the just pre-Chippendale period in furniture design, c. 1750. The lower two thirds of the centre splat are formed as a classical vase, pierced to represent lobing, surmounted by a pair of raffle leaves below a 'c' scroll escutcheon and a gadroon moulded top rail, which at each end lifts the spirits of the viewer.

BACK COVER IMAGE
A mahogany and marquetry serpentine sideboard, fitted with drawer and cupboard compartments developed from a serving table, c. 1790.

PAGE 2 IMAGE
A mid-Victorian calamander, satinwood, purplewood and ivory marquetry side cabinet by Holland and Sons with marquetry designs after Owen Jones ,1870. See also page 95.

ACKNOWLEDGEMENTS

I am indebted to my dear friend Eric Knowles for his industrious and scholarly input. Revising and bringing up to date any book is arguably harder than writing anew, and Eric has done a masterful job with his customary flare. I would also like to thank Mary Greensted for her assistance in creating some of the later captions.

All unattributed Illustrations are courtesy of Bonhams Auctioneers unless otherwise credited.

CONTENTS

INTRODUCTION

FURNITURE is the one commodity that has been found in every household, worldwide, since the beginning of civilisation. Its form, manufacture and finesse are linked inextricably to political, international and social history. If you enjoy discovering how our forebears lived and worked at every social level, there can be no better way than through the study of their furniture, which both offered them convenience and embellished their homes.

In the past, the story of old English furniture has been divided into five main periods: Elizabethan, Jacobean or Carolean, Georgian, Regency and Victorian. To a certain extent, these coincided with the introduction of newly fashionable timber – chronologically, oak, walnut, mahogany and satinwood, although during the Regency and Victorian periods, all suitable timbers were used at one time or another.

More recently, a greater degree of accuracy has been necessary, and these labels have been sub-divided, sometimes under the name of a monarch, sometimes under the name of a leading maker, designer or architect.

One area that has facilitated research on furniture is the popularity of period costume drama for both film and television, enabling production companies to pay location fees to stately homes and houses. This has made money available to employ professional archivists to painstakingly forage through generations of old manuscripts, documents, letters and ephemera to reveal names and other details of suppliers of everything from farm equipment to fine furniture and household effects, goods and chattels. Thus positive proof of the dates of manufacture have been established, whereas before only supposition and opinion held sway.

One problem has hitherto been the question of pieces made 'out of period'. Items made seventy or eighty years after an original to replace a loss due to damage or theft, or made to augment a single or a set. These have been puzzle pieces, for if they are careful copies it is extremely difficult to determine precisely when they were made. But having traced one such piece to a date in a specific collection, a similar connection may be made to another. In this fascinating aspect, research continues.

Antique furniture, from whatever period and whatever part of the world, is now seen much more as an important way to look seriously at social history and the broader picture of environs of the past. Each era displays for us its unique style in architecture, music, dress, etiquette, landscape gardening and fine and decorative arts. All are inter-related and to fully appreciate one there must be a basic understanding of the rest.

Because furniture is basically functional, we think of it as conforming to certain types; tables, chairs, cabinets etc. But unlike most other household items there is another field entirely; the piece custom made specifically for a purpose which we may never discover. For example, a table with a strange shape to the top or an additional flap with no support, an unexplained hole or a brass mount with no fixture. For these many reasons and more the study of English furniture can become a lifetime's passion.

Opposite:
The Drawing Room, designed by James Wyatt (1746–1813), Castle Coole, County Fermanagh, Northern Ireland. The form of decoration on the sofa is a magnificent example of the rococo revival of the 1820s. As it incorporates everything imaginable from the first sixty years of the eighteenth century, it is often referred to as 'Tous les Louis'. (National Trust Photographic Library / Patrick Prendergast / The Bridgeman Art Library.)

Chapter One

THE SIXTEENTH CENTURY

TUDOR, 1500–58

BY THE YEAR 1500, England's first Tudor King, Henry VII, had brought a period of unity and stability to a previously troubled land. The entire country had a population of just five million – less than that of Greater London today. England had been renowned for centuries for high quality workmanship in both building and decorating. For the most part, such skills were applied to work for the church. Large secular houses constructed before the reign of Henry VII had been sturdily built and heavily fortified. They were meant to look awesome and impenetrable and the furniture therein was sparse and utilitarian. The family home did not so much give the impression of a permanent gathering together of possessions under a single roof, but almost of 'camping' in a building with household goods that could be rapidly collected together and moved if the family should be under attack. To create expensively and ornately furnished homes would have been foolish at a time when it might all be for nothing if an attack was launched by a hostile neighbour. A family's wealth was displayed by the fineness of the banners and other wall hangings. It was also evident in the amount of silverware and gold on display and, of course, in the quality of blankets and bedding, all of which could be packed into a chest at short notice and carried to safety.

However, as Henry VII brought stability to the land, all this was set to change and an era of English furniture was born. This was the age of oak. Not just English oak which, with its natural stout curving branches and short trunk, was much used for building ships and houses. To supplement our dwindling supply, oak was brought from Norway and the Baltic, too. In more remote parts of the country, essential furniture was made from ash, elm, beech or English fruitwood, but, because these were less durable than oak, little from this period has survived.

Although fireplaces had existed since the thirteenth century, the archaic practice of lighting a fire in the middle of the room, so that the smoke drifted upwards to a barn-like roof to escape where it could, persisted in many of the old baronial houses. The dining table would be placed at the high end of the hall. The master and mistress of the house sat at the centre of the table with their guests and members of the household on their right and left respectively, all facing the fire. With the exception of the hosts, who had throne-like seats with high backs and solid arms, everyone else sat on stools or benches, using the wall for back-support.

Like the wall hangings, silverware and so on, tables and benches were also made with portability in mind. Collapsible, portable and expendable were the key requirements for the carpenters who produced furniture, and remained so until the

Opposite:
The Great Hall at Trerice.
The plasterwork was
extensively restored in
about 1840. The room is
set faithfully as it would
have been, with the
fashionable and thus
popular court-cupboard to
the left of the door. It was
an Elizabethan form and
takes its name from
the French court,
meaning short in
contrast to the earlier
long cupboards.
(Country Life Picture
Library)

An oak linen-fold chest from the mid-sixteenth century. This style of low relief carving was popular in the sixteenth century.

An early sixteenth-century oak dole cupboard, showing Gothic tracery designs. (Haddon Hall / The Bridgeman Art Library)

A six-plank oak coffer from the late sixteenth to early seventeenth century. The 'V' in the side planks makes the four legs.

mid-sixteenth century, when the stability hard-won by his father was disturbed by Henry VIII, culminating in the monumental break with the Roman Catholic Church and the dissolution of the monasteries. Churches, abbeys and priories throughout the land were despoiled and fittings, windows, memorials, floors, wall paintings, alabaster figures and thousands of ounces of fine silverware were destroyed.

The small amount of decoration which generally appeared on early domestic furniture at this time took its theme from ecclesiastic or Gothic style, particularly the arch shapes of doors and windows. Such decoration was achieved by carving in low relief, and many early chests bore the kind of chip-carving embellishment where the surface of the wood was cut away in small, regular chunks to form the pattern. The most common use for this type of carving was on the outer edges of a piece, the main parts being left plain. After applying a grain filler, furniture was often painted with a kind of tempera. The affinity of sacred and secular designs, particularly on chests, remained well into the sixteenth century, especially in rural England.

Most domestic furniture construction used a basic plank or slab method, the six-plank coffer being a typical example. Two equal pieces of wood formed each end, three more formed the front, back and base and a sixth made the top. The two ends were often cut with a large inverted V to make four simple feet and the joints were secured with large, hand-made nails or pegs. The dining table, however, had now evolved from two or three long planks joined to form a loose top resting on two or three trestles, to a table top fixed to a framed base.

The joints of the frame were made with a tongue (tenon) on one piece fitting into a pre-cut slot (mortice) in the other – the mortice and tenon joint. The joints were dry, that is, without glue, and allowed sufficient movement for the wood to expand and contract without cracking, but were tight enough to form a secure structure.

A 'joined' or joint stool from the sixteenth to seventeenth century. The pegged joints can clearly be seen.

The construction of a mortice and tenon joint. Originally called a 'mortesse and tennant', the latter part fitted into a precut slot in which one or two holes had been bored. The tenon was marked, removed, and then bored with two holes off centre from those in the mortice. When placed together again, split willow pegs were driven in to secure the joint.

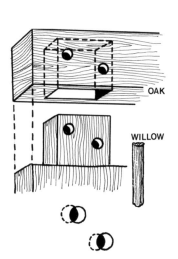

OAK

WILLOW

Before being finally put together, one or two holes were bored in the mortice and tenon parts, slightly off centre from each other so that when joined in place, an incomplete circle could be seen when looking through the joint. A wooden peg was then driven into this aperture forcing the two parts tightly together. Willow was mostly used for this process because it has a long, fibrous grain and when split (not cut) into pegs, and driven into position, a willow-pegged joint is almost impossible to break. This construction enabled the insertion or inclusion of a thin panel of wood within a frame to create a side to a piece of furniture far lighter in weight than had been previously possible. It was a revolutionary development that changed furniture making for ever. The use of panelling and joining furniture has remained integral and the man responsible for the frame-making was (and still is) known as a 'joyner', or joiner. One important means of authenticating a piece of early furniture made by this method is to look underneath and inside the frame at the ends of the pegs, which had been driven in from the outside. They were rarely cut off and so protrude up to half an inch inside the frame. This only applied to the underside of seat rails and other places where, in normal use, they would not be seen or cause an obstruction. This practice continued well into the eighteenth century in England and even later in Europe.

The tradition of designing and manufacturing easily portable furniture continued during the religious persecution and general unrest under the Council of Regency of the young Edward VI (reigned 1547–53) who died aged 16, and under his half-sister Queen Mary (reigned 1553–8).

By the accession of Elizabeth I in 1558, new ideas of design were slowly being absorbed from abroad. The revival of classical forms that had begun in Italy in the fifteenth century (*rinascimento* in Italian, *renaissance* in French) began to affect English design. Ecclesiastical commissions were at a standstill because of the upheavals in the church and craftsmen turned their skills to domestic work. During the latter part of the sixteenth century they were encouraged by a more peaceful England and a settled home life. One example of direct Italian Renaissance influence was the shape of the so-called savonarola folding chair. Such chairs became popular throughout Europe from the late 1400s, and remained so until the twentieth century. The chair got its name in the Victorian period as a marketing label, evoking Girolamo Savonarola, a Dominican friar introduced to Florence by Lorenzo Medici and who, ironically, was to preach strongly against the Medici family and the Renaissance while still under Lorenzo's patronage. English chairs of the sixteenth century in shape of the savonarola are extremely rare, but the chair was much copied in the United Kingdom during the latter part of the nineteenth century, so beware!

ELIZABETHAN, 1558–1603

The reign of Queen Elizabeth brought a new age of prosperity and internal peace. A new middle-class emerged – businessmen and tradesmen who were determined that their families should enjoy the same stable and secure family life that had previously been the prerogative only of the rich. In larger households, servants and other members of the retinue no longer shared food, wine or enjoyed entertainment with the family. Instead they had their own quarters and their own simple furniture, which in time became a vital part of the growth of the furniture industry. With the different patterns of life, different patterns of furniture naturally developed.

A sixteenth-century Elizabethan oak dining table with double cup or cup and cover supports. The bulbous legs and low horizontal stretchers are typical of the period.

The great hall, now often called the dining chamber, became much more as we would recognise it with the fireplace and chimney in one wall of the room, whilst the dining table was often placed in the centre of the room. Although still long and rectangular in shape, the joined frames now comprised four or six bulbous, turned legs, connected by horizontal members or stretchers, the lower ones six to eight inches from the floor and those at the top forming a frieze rail or apron. On finer furniture, the frieze rails were often decorated with carving or simple types of inlay, which was just coming into vogue. Stools and benches were often made and decorated to match the table and were placed all around it. Two legs of a stool were extended upwards to form a back and 'back-stools' became fashionable. Thus the chair for dining became established as an article of domestic furniture.

As furniture became more ornate and diverse in use, more skill was needed in its manufacture. In London and other major cities, joining, turning and carving were often the separate occupations of individual craftsmen, while in the country all three were often required of a single highly skilled man who was known as a 'bodger'. In contrast to today's meaning of the word, the bodger and his work were highly regarded and much in demand. Turning was done with a pole lathe set beside a springy young tree. A rope would be attached to its topmost tip. The piece to be turned would be mounted in a simple lathe, the rope wound around it and the end attached to a treadle on the floor. The spring in the tree pulled the rope up, and pressure on the treadle pulled it down, causing the wood to spin first one way and then the other. Turning by this method continued in some parts of England until well into the nineteenth century, and the majority of pre-1800 fruitwood, yew and beech turned parts, such as legs, stretchers, spindles, chair backs and cupboard door panels were made in this way. It is encouraging to see that there is now a revival of wood-turning, both by machine and pole lathe.

By the end of the sixteenth century, people needed all sorts of hitherto unknown furniture for their homes. As this furniture evolved, new terms to describe it entered the English vocabulary. An early example is 'dresser', a board on which the servants 'dressed' the night's food in case the master of the house suffered from night starvation! Another is 'cupboard'. Cups were traditionally a sign of wealth and cupboards were literally what they sounded like – surfaces on which cups could be displayed and stored – and only later were they enclosed for security, although the word remained unchanged. The term 'buffet' comes from the French *beau fête,* meaning a place where a grand epicurean display of food could be mounted. Food and clothes cupboards with doors that swung open on two iron pivots, many with panels of turned spindles forming a grille, also appeared. These were known as 'livery cupboards' or 'aumbries' and there were several variations. Some were small and set on an open 'joined' stand; others were tall enough to conceal a person. Of the cupboard on a stand type the two most popular were the buffet or 'court' cupboard and the hall cupboard. One feature common to nearly all these is that the top part was set back a little to create a narrow shelf, whilst the top rail (see page 23 illustration) protrudes in line with the base to form a canopy. In almost all the earlier pieces, this was supported by a bulbous turned column at each front corner, probably matching the turned legs of the dining table, stools and chairs.

The front or foot posts of Elizabethan beds were similarly turned. They supported one end of the ceiling or canopy over the bed, while the other end rested on a carved and inlaid headboard. This type of bed is known as a 'full tester', that is, fully covered. It was hung with fine cloth drapes and tapestry curtains to offer warmth and privacy, a cosy room within a vaster one. At various times in history, this canopy was adapted to extend over only half the bed, when it is known as a 'half tester'.

It was during the Elizabethan period that furniture decoration came to the fore, with elaborate turning and further enrichment with inlay. To create this, the piece of wood to be decorated would have a pattern, usually of stylised flowers, vines, tendrils and leaves, drawn onto it. This would then be cut out of the wood, usually to the depth of about a quarter of an inch. Using these pieces as 'patterns', the same shapes would be drawn on to, and then cut out of, woods contrasting in colour, such as holly, box or ebony, and the pieces carefully let into the appropriate section of wood to be decorated. Occasionally ivory or mother-of-pearl were incorporated. This type of inlay became the popular decoration for rails, friezes and frames on all top quality furniture, as well as for complete panelled rooms. The main themes were either 'foliate', as described, or geometric, wherein small, symmetrical pieces of wood in alternating colours were used, called 'chequer' inlay.

A seventeenth-century oak tester bed with bulbous front supports from Towneley Hall, Burnley. A full tester bed with bulbous cup-and-cover posts at the foot and inlaid panels at the head. This form became popular during the late Elizabethan period and is usually associated with it, but examples are found dating from the early seventeenth century.

Chapter Two

THE SEVENTEENTH CENTURY

JAMES I, 1603–25

WITH THE ACCESSION of James I of England (James VI of Scotland) came the Jacobean period. James was the first King of England, Scotland, Wales and Ireland but, unlike Elizabeth and many of his successors, he had little personal influence on style or design of furniture.

One significant change in a particular motif was the gradual elongation of the bulbous 'double cup' or 'cup and cover' leg or support, creating an almost vase-like shape, while its carved decoration became deeper and more foliate in style. At the same time, a variety of different patterns for the turner emerged including bobbin turning, which looks like a number of balls joined together in a straight line, sometimes interspersed with rings. Like the other experimental patterns it demanded a careful choice of timber, for although at first it was used only for legs and rails, complete chairs were soon made with every member turned in this pattern and long-grained wood was needed for strength. This led to another innovative discovery. Turned wood columns could be cut in half lengthways and then applied to the carcase – the basic framework of chest furniture – as well as to drawer fronts and doors as decoration. To compensate for the saw cut and ensure a complete half-circular section, the wood was first cut in half and the two sections fastened together before being turned. This type of decoration was popular for a relatively short time prior to the Civil War and remained popular throughout most of the seventeenth century.

It was during the early seventeenth century that the usefulness of a piece of furniture with several sliding drawers became apparent. However, when the drawers were full, their weight caused them to rub on the supporting rail in the carcase. So the drawer bottom was made to extend beyond the width of the drawer, the resultant two 'lips' running into slots cut into the carcase. To hide the slots when the drawer was in place, the drawer-front was made larger than the opening in the carcase. It was not long before two proper drawer runners were added. Each runner was a strip of hard wood, approximately three quarters of an inch by half an inch, placed in the carcase or body of the piece midway between the top and bottom of the drawer opening at each side and running from front to back. A groove, called a 'rabbet' was then worked into the sides of the drawer to accommodate the runner. Thus the drawer was 'suspended' and could be used without stress to the carcase frame. This highly efficient construction was discontinued and replaced by runners at each bottom edge to the sides as furniture became finer and lighter during the early 1700s. The newly fashionable thin drawer linings allowed no room for the in-cut rabbet. With the exception of one

Opposite:
The Cartoon Gallery at Knole House, Sevenoaks, Kent. The fine upholstery with deep bobble fringes and ornate, and complex carving to the walnut frames, identify the chairs and stools as dating from around 1685. (National Trust Photographic Library/Andreas von Einsiedel/The Bridgeman Art Library.)

Five types of turned and carved supports used on chairs, stools and tables during the seventeenth century. The following approximate dates are when these designs were most popular. (a) Knob or bobbin turning, 1630–75. (b) Ball and ring or bobbin turning, 1640–75. (c) Double cup or cup and cover, often carved with fluting, 1580–1690. (d) Fluted baluster, 1600–1700. (e) Pillar, 1605–75.

or two out-of-date provincial pieces, the next time we see the suspended drawer on English furniture is in the twentieth century.

Previously, drawers had seldom been used in any piece other than the base parts of buffets but now, thanks to the development of runners, a single long drawer or two short drawers side by side were being built into the bases of chest furniture. Part chest, part drawers, such pieces became very popular and, because of the hybrid construction, became known as 'mule' chests. Extremely fine examples can be found dating from the mid-eighteenth century, but their popularity declined after 1820.

Sliding, movable parts in furniture gave us the extending, or draw-leaf, dining table. First introduced in Elizabethan times, this type of table reached a peak of popularity during the Jacobean era, but went out of fashion during the first 25 years of the eighteenth century. It was revived in a modified form by Thomas Sheraton in the 1790s and the mechanism has remained in use to the present date. When closed, the table looks like a refectory or long dining table with a double top on a rectangular frame, supported by four or six turned legs. The top lifts up, and from each end a leaf of timber the same width and thickness, and almost half the length of the top, is pulled out. Each of these leaves has attached to the underside two 'lopers', or extended runners, the same length as the table. When both leaves are pulled out, the centre part drops down level with the two leaves and its weight, pressing on the four lopers, supports the two ends.

During the early 1600s, the 'moulded front' on drawer, door and chest panels was added to the list of new features that began to replace previously popular carved 'linen-fold' effect. Panels carved in low relief giving the appearance of a folded piece of cloth had been used for sacred and secular furniture for more than a hundred years. It is important to note that linen-fold had gone out of fashion by the 1640s, not to

A seventeenth-century mule chest, subsequently so called because the single low drawer made it neither pure coffer nor pure chest of drawers

return until the Victorian revival of the 1860s. To create a moulded front, the drawer was set back about ¾ of an inch in the carcase frame. Four strips of wood were then applied round the edge, forming a frame. The strips were of triangular section and the longest side was moulded or grooved. Another piece of wood of the same proportions as the drawer front, but smaller, was then applied to the centre. This piece might be up to 1½ inches thick and was framed with more moulding; in the centre of this went the metal handle. The more elaborate chests of the 1620–40 period had complex variations on this symmetrical moulded theme. A typical example is the chest with one long, deep drawer, moulded to simulate two short drawers above two cupboard doors

This sort of linen-fold carving was losing popularity by the first half of the seventeenth century, to be replaced by moulded fronts.

similarly decorated and enclosing three plain-fronted drawers. The two doors were secured by an iron lock and swung open on iron hinges. A substantial piece of moulding was then added immediately below the drawer or door opening at the base of the carcase to balance the overhanging top and the whole article was raised from the floor by the elongated upright corner members of the carcase.

By the early 1620s, an improved method of joining the front of a drawer to the sides had been devised, while the back joints were still secured by iron nails in the established manner. The new method was known as 'dove-tailing' because of the shape of the parts to be joined. On the earliest, provincial examples of dove-tailing, the larger joints were strengthened with an iron pin. However, the rapid refinement of joiners' skills, and the introduction of new materials during the following twenty years, dispensed with the need for this nailing on the finest furniture, but it is often found on country-made pieces as late as the beginning of the eighteenth century.

CHARLES I, 1625–49

Unlike James I, Charles I was a connoisseur and a patron of art. He had immense personal influence on style and fashion and his marriage to Henrietta, daughter of Henry IV of France, increased considerably the English desire for Continental design, fashion and etiquette. He is acknowledged as the first collector of works of art from other countries as well as England. He was fond of, and advocated, reading, hitherto confined to lay scholars and the clergy. This meant the gradual appearance of library furniture in more important households, as well as in educational and ecclesiastical establishments. He encouraged the development of trade with Europe and the Middle and Far East through the English East India Company. This company had been incorporated by royal charter in 1600 to compete with the Dutch merchants for trade in lands beyond the Cape of Good Hope or the Strait of Magellan, and so began an age of great commercial expansion.

As the requirements of household furniture became rapidly more diverse, more accuracy was necessary in its manufacture, and coinciding with this was the more general use of walnut, much of which was imported from Spain and the south of France. Until the latter part of the seventeenth century, walnut was used in the solid and because it had a much closer grain than oak, it could be cut with much more precision. When well rubbed down by hand-polishing, it showed great depth of colour and extremely attractive markings.

By the early 1640s fine porcelain was being imported from China, glass from Venice, pottery from Delft in Holland, spices and peppers from the East Indies and fine cloth from Damascus and Italy. Fine leathers from Europe, cane from the Orient and chests or trunks from Japan, decorated with lacquer and known as 'japanned' work, were among several new imports that were to have a tremendous influence on the development of English furniture.

Portrait of King Charles I at his trial. The King sits on an upholstered chair – rare at this time. (Philip Mould Ltd, London/The Bridgeman Art Library)

An oak chest with arcade carved front, 1650.

Covering and padding chairs was rare before 1645 and, apart from at Court and in the wealthiest households, costly upholstered chairs were kept in the bedroom where they were unlikely to be worn by frequent use. The few upholstered chairs designed for use elsewhere were of square and solid shape, the back legs splayed out to counteract the inborn habit of all generations to tip back, and with a low back. This was popularly used to accommodate the arm of the gentleman as he sat sideways, thus unencumbered by his sword. (The practice of leaving personal armaments in an ante-room whilst paying social calls was not instituted until the early eighteenth century.) Equally, they offered an unrestricted seat for a lady wearing the fashionable voluminous skirt and underframe, hence the name 'farthingale' chair.

England was expanding internationally in global trade and commerce, but such rapid growth slowed dramatically when the country was divided by civil war. This led to the execution of Charles I and the exile of his sons, Charles and James, to France. The eleven years of the Commonwealth which followed under the government of Oliver Cromwell, 1649–60, was a period of overriding religious zeal and for the most part the development and advancement of design was a matter of chance rather than intention.

COMMONWEALTH, 1649–60

For innovators, designers and those with aesthetic aspirations, the 1650s were notoriously lean, dull and dismal where furniture and indeed any of the arts were concerned. Puritan beliefs decreed self-denial in all things; goods and chattels were to be made strictly functional, without unnecessary adornment and with precious little comfort. Furniture made in the south of England and in the Midlands particularly during this time reflects this feeling. Cupboards and chests were joined and panelled without carving or inlay; at most a simple gouged line around the edges of the frame was sometimes used. Legs for tables and chairs had the simplest of turning, often of plain tapering form, severe but elegant. Abroad, however, two

Above:
Whitehouse signpost barometer c. 1820, being an interesting revival of one of the earliest original forms of barometer.

Right:
A late seventeenth-century marquetry longcase clock with 10-inch dial by Benjamin Willoughby of Bristol. Marquetry was a popular form of decoration on all manner of furniture between 1695 and 1720.

Far right:
An example of a Torricellian or cistern barometer, better known as a stick barometer. Invented in the late seventeenth century, this mahogany example dates to the mid eighteenth century.

Opposite top:
A seventeenth-century oak hall cupboard showing turned pendants below the canopy. See also page 14.

men were working on experiments that were to create new exercises for the skills of our English craftsmen in the good times to come.

While putting into practice a theory by Galileo in 1643, fellow Italian Evangelista Torricelli discovered that the external atmosphere controls the power of a vacuum inside a sealed tube. If a glass tube has a measured amount of mercury (which is a non-evaporative liquid metal until heated) poured into it and is sealed, the rise and fall of the mercury will indicate the external atmosphere or barometric pressure. Torricelli was hampered for a while by the lack of sufficiently advanced materials, the most important being suitable glass tubing, but concurrent improvements within the glass-making industry quickly remedied this and he had opened the way towards the invention of the first domestic barometer. A major development occurred in 1670 when Sir Samuel Morland produced a signpost barometer. The bend in the tube extends about 12 inches and rises off the horizontal about 3 inches, thereby showing with greater accuracy any atmospheric change along, rather than up and down, the tube. Examples are rare, for this type did not gain the popularity expected, wealthy clients preferring the simpler stick or pillar type of case, which continued to be made for the next two hundred years, with its decoration following the style of the different periods. In turn, this was superseded in general popularity toward the end of the eighteenth century by the banjo or wheel barometer, but it returned to favour during the latter part of the nineteenth century.

Another key figure in contemporary science and astronomy was Christiaan Huygens, a Dutchman, who in 1657 made the remarkable discovery of the importance of the applied pendulum. This was originally yet another of Galileo's theories, but he had used it only in researching oscillations. By giving a pendulum momentum by means of power from a weight on a chain or specially woven rope over a toothed wheel, and correcting the length of the arc of its swing by means of a mechanical escapement, it was possible to achieve accuracy with a timepiece movement. Thus began the refinement of the clock, which, in its various forms was soon to become one of the most desirable items of furniture in the finer houses all over England.

RESTORATION AND CAROLEAN, 1660–85

When Charles II landed at Dover in May 1660, a whole new, bright and optimistic atmosphere lifted the spirits of the English. As the new king was crowned at Westminster in April 1661, and married Catherine of Braganza the following year, the country once more celebrated in the *joie de vivre* that reflected the character of their new ruler.

Charles II was quick witted, a man of great and varied knowledge and a shrewd judge of character. He also enjoyed an active love life: after Lady Castlemaine, his two long-term mistresses, from opposite ends of the social scale, were the French courtier Louise de Kerouaille, later to become the Duchess of Portsmouth, and Nell Gwynne. He loved his illegitimate children, his dogs, his ducks and his Navy. He found pleasure in theatre-going, horse racing, gambling and at the same time patronised the arts and the sciences and encouraged trade with Europe and the East.

Below:
An oak chest of drawers from 1660 showing the new fashion for geometric moulded fronts and raised panel drawers. See also page 19.

The new freedom released by Charles II's *mode vivant* goes some way towards explaining how so many innovations in design and uses of furniture came to be crammed into the next twenty-five years. What Charles II patronised in life, his courtiers, the noblemen, landed gentry and so on down the social scale, followed as far as their means permitted. Interest in all forms of the arts and sciences was revived. As well as paintings and *objets d'art*, people started collecting porcelain, pottery, glass and books and it became fashionable to be the proud owner of one of the new-fangled clocks or barometers. And so a new type of furniture was required to house and display these possessions – case or cabinet furniture.

It became obvious that the panels in the doors of cupboards should be of glass (for the while, still imported from Venice) instead

of wood, so that the prized collections could be displayed and admired whilst at the same time being protected against dust, damage and theft. However, the old method of joining and allowing room for the wood to 'move' proved inappropriate for glass panels, which did not expand or contract. Therefore, it became necessary to construct frames with the joints cut to a higher degree of accuracy. The demand became so great that a new craftsman emerged who specialised in the manufacture of case and cabinet furniture – the cabinet-maker. In time, he would be called upon to supply all manner of cases, cupboards and cabinets, some with glazed doors, some with mirrors, others solid or 'blind', finely carved or decorated with highly figured veneers, marquetry, parquetry and even lacquer and gilding. His title is now much used, often misused, and synonymous with all manufacture and even repairs, but originally it described the elite of the furniture industry.

In 1663, George Villiers, second Duke of Buckingham, secured the sole right to manufacture mirror plates of silvered glass, which he quite unjustly claimed was a process hitherto unknown in England. He set up a factory at Vauxhall and brought over glassmakers from Italy, the centre of the glass industry, to assist him in establishing large-scale production. Several other patents and monopolies appear to have been granted at the same time and, as the output of mirror glasses grew, so did the need for decorative frames to surround them. Many materials were used, such as metal, ivory, tortoiseshell and even needlework over a wood base, which in the early period was often of 'cushion' form and lasted until the early years of the eighteenth century.

During the 1660s, large quantities of cane were imported from the East. It was found that, when woven and strung across seats and backs of chairs, cane provided a lighter, cheaper seat which was also extremely comfortable. Charles II is recorded

Below:
A late seventeenth-century gilt wood wall mirror with pierced frame, carved with amorini amongst flowering plants.

Below right:
A seventeenth-century beadwork mirror worked with figures of a king and queen beneath draped tent canopies, and exotic beasts, birds and insects, all within a tortoiseshell moulded banded frame.

as having some folding cane-seated chairs for his tents on Hounslow Heath. Caning chairs soon became a cottage as well as a workshop industry and the output was enormous. This is why it is still possible to find some fine examples of cane panel seat furniture made during the last quarter of the seventeenth century at comparatively moderate prices. Perhaps the most common of these is the high-back walnut chair, which can be used as either a dining or hall chair. Such chairs are easy to date accurately because of the extreme changes in shape which they underwent, almost year by year, from 1660 to 1685. The 'H' stretcher frame for chairs became very popular during the early Restoration period, whereas the cross member came slightly more to the front on later examples. Pierced carving on the back, top and side rails also became popular and was adopted for the decoration of the Dutch Bow front rail during the 1680s. Also from Holland, where Charles had spent much of his exile, came the Flemish curve, which started to appear on the front legs of furniture, especially chairs. This was often combined with the scroll foot, also known as the 'Braganza foot', a Spanish influence honouring the Queen.

There was another major reason for the unprecedented production of state-of-the-art furniture during the reign of Charles II. In 1666, the Great Fire of London destroyed 13,200 homes. As these were rebuilt, the finest were refurnished in the latest styles of the period and cabinet-makers, chair-makers, turners and joiners were all gainfully employed supplying this sudden demand.

Joiners made carcase and chest pieces as well as a new and large variety of tables, while chair makers and turners made chairs, day-beds and settles as well as turned posts for tables, buffets and four-poster beds. The day-bed, which derived from the French chaise longue, first appeared in England during the early Restoration period. It was constructed in the same manner as the contemporary chair but with a seat that extended forward some five feet and sometimes with an adjustable back-rest.

Another interesting facet of English furniture making which emerged at this time was the demand for smaller articles of furniture made for a specific purpose, such as the escritoire. A development of the early writing desk with a sloping top and a forerunner of the bureau, the escritoire was rare in England before the middle of the seventeenth century, but its considerable use is recorded after the Restoration. Basically formed as a desk with a space to accommodate the knees of the writer and in some instances with a flap that could be raised to form a larger surface, a small drawer was often incorporated in the frieze of the stand. The design of the stand inevitably followed the latest developments in the art of the turner. One such development during this period was 'barley sugar twist' turning. This design, which is self-descriptive, remained popular in the provinces until well in to the eighteenth century but had disappeared from stylish furniture by the early 1700s. (It was again popular in the mid- to late-Victorian period.) Barley sugar twist turning was a difficult operation for the seventeenth-century turner until the introduction of the 'sliding rest'

A chair rail of bow form of the 1680s, shown here with the Braganza foot. During this period the H stretcher on this type of frame chair was sometimes replaced by an elaborate curving X.

on the lathe. This enabled the turner to rest his hand and turning chisel on a bracket which slid along parallel with the piece of wood to be turned. Imagine gouging a line along a circular piece of wood, left to right. If the wood is being rotated while the line is being gouged, the result will be a line encircling the wood from end to end. The speed of the gouge as it is drawn from one end of wood to the other together with the speed of the lathe determines the length of the spiral and either heavy or fine barley sugar turning is produced.

Barley sugar turning formed the legs and stretchers of many of the chairs and gate-leg tables of the 1660–85 period, as well as those for the chests and cabinets-on-stands which were becoming so popular. A cabinet, containing possibly a dozen small deep drawers enclosed by two large doors, was placed on an open-framed stand which often had a drawer in the frieze. Alternatively, the two doors were replaced by one large one that was hinged at the bottom, rather than at the sides, and so fell down and forward, forming a writing surface supported by chains or steel arms to create another form of escritoire.

There were innovations in table-making during this period, too. The single-flap tables of around 1660 developed into two-flap oval, round, rectangular and square tables. The two flaps or 'leaves' were attached to the centre with simple iron hinges,

Below:
A walnut side chair of the Restoration period featuring a cane-work back and seat, 1665.

Below right:
A fine Charles II period side chair with pierced panels to the back and front stretcher rail. Note the early use of cane to the seat and back.

folding down when not in use. The central part was on a rectangular frame with a leg at each corner and a square framed leg set in each long side. This swung out on a pivot joint from the main rectangle and, because its outside upright member was the same length as the four main legs, it served to support the flap, or drop leaf. Because of its construction, this kind of table became generally known as a 'gate-leg' table, although not all tables of this period had a completely framed 'gate'.

At the court of Charles II, gambling had become a fashionable pastime, so gaming tables became another obligatory piece of furniture in a rich man's house, offering another new challenge to the joiner. During the last quarter of the seventeenth century, card games of loo, basset, ombre and quadrille (ombre for four) were played for high stakes, as well as chess, backgammon and dicing. Card games were played best on tables covered with green cloth or fine needlework. Coincidentally protecting this when not in use, the table tops were hinged to fold over in half, supported when open by one or two legs being made to swing out from the frame in the manner of the earlier gate-leg. When closed, the table showed a solid wood surface and could stand against the wall to be used as an additional side table.

It was at this point that the fashion for Continental travel exerted its greatest influence to date, and the work of the carver and gilder came to the fore as they were called upon to replicate the exuberance of the French, German and Italian

Above:
A writing desk or escritoire c. 1695. The two inside front legs swing out to support the sloping fall, making more room for the knees of the sitter.

Left:
A seventeenth-century day bed from Towneley Hall, Burnley. Day beds were first introduced in England during the first half of the sixteenth century.

A small oak gate-leg table from c. 1675. The legs are shown extended to support the leaves.

baroque designs. These forces continued to exert great influence throughout the seventeenth, eighteenth and nineteenth centuries.

The skills of the carver were well displayed with the continuing use of walnut, as can be seen in the fret, or through cutting and shaping on the chairs of the period. But this work was even more in demand with the fashion for gilding and silvering the surface of carved furniture. As the carved wood was to be covered, there was no need to use expensive walnut. Cheaper, softer woods were quite adequate, and pine and lime were found to be superior materials for the carvers' work. They also formed a sound basis for the foundation layer of gesso prior to the application of the gold or silver leaf itself.

Gesso is a combination of pure fine chalk and size (made from scrapings of parchment) mixed together to make a paste. It had been applied to the surface of furniture as a grain-filler since the middle ages, but during the seventeenth century its full potential in the hands of a skilled carver was finally realised. Deep open carving could be coated with layers of gesso, each being allowed to dry before the application of the next. This then formed a surface as hard and, when well rubbed down, as smooth as ivory. The carver could add emphasis to his work by carving further fine detail into the gesso before the article was sent to the gilder. Several coats of burnish size were applied and allowed to harden before the gilder wet the surface with water and then applied the pure gold leaf. Because the burnish size quickly absorbed the moisture, only small areas could be gilded at one time, thus making the achievement of a consistent colour and surface on large pieces a highly skilled and lengthy process. When the whole had been covered with gold, it was rubbed well with a pad, making the surface dull or 'matt'. It was then ready for the finishing stage, when protruding parts of the carving were burnished to a mirror-like surface, thus gaining the 'highlights'. This work (see illustration page 81) was carried out with a dog's tooth or later a polished agate stone correctly shaped and set into a convenient handle. The two main methods of gilding furniture are water gilding, described above, and oil gilding, when oil rather than water is a constituent of the gesso. The latter is used more architecturally and on iron-work and cannot be burnished. Oil gilding is generally considered less suitable for fine furniture decoration.

Applying a precious metal to a cheap one for aggrandisement was an ancient craft, and fire or mercurial gilding had been used to decorate metals since the middle ages. To obtain the gilded finish, mercury and gold were mixed to form an amalgam; this was applied to the surface of the metal and the article and then heated. The mercury evaporates and leaves a gold coating. Gilded metal mounts on the finest specimen pieces of furniture were standard by the beginning of the seventeenth century.

The chinoiserie taste of the Carolean period made itself apparent in furniture with the considerable use of japanned or lacquered decoration. The appearance of japanned work is of scenes wherein the figures, birds, flowers and other main characters are slightly raised from the background surface and then decorated with colour and/or gold leaf. At this time vast quantities of lacquered panels and pieces of furniture were being imported from the East, but demand for the new lacquer-ware so exceeded supply that it was obviously necessary to attempt to produce such furniture in England. However, craftsmen could not obtain the essential ingredients to make the lacquer, nor was there the right climate or physical temperament for its application, for lacquer hardens in a humid atmosphere and it is painstakingly slow. Eventually, frustrated English craftsmen began to copy the effect as best they could. In 1668, John Stalker and George Parker produced *A Treatise of Japanning and Varnishing*, an important and comprehensive work giving full directions and details concerning surface decoration of furniture, particularly in the Oriental manner. Instead of gum from the lac tree, they suggested using a variety of varnishes and other materials and, whereas the background of the seventeenth-century Oriental lacquer was invariably black, English lacquer of the same period was produced with red, yellow, green and blue backgrounds.

We can assume that, when new, both English and Oriental lacquer looked nearly the same, but as the methods of their preparation and application were so totally different, they have reacted to the passing of time in noticeably different ways. Where seventeenth-century English lacquer has chipped and come away from the surface, it has done so in the outline of the raised parts, making obvious the shape and size of the character now missing. Oriental lacquer of the same period, however, tends to come away in irregular-sized pieces.

Both English and Oriental lacquer cabinets, enclosed chests and trunks were popular in England until the early eighteenth century and often placed on specially made carved and gilded wood stands. As these were usually in the current European style, the combination created a quite dramatic contrast; the restrained and elegant upper part on its ornately carved and gilded base.

Stimulated by the works of Inigo Jones (1573–1652) in the reign of Charles I, a taste for architecture in the classical tradition according to the ancient and noble

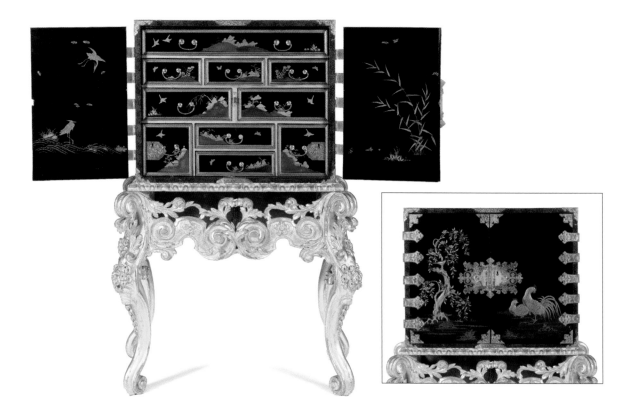

An Oriental lacquer cabinet on a carved and gilt wood stand, c. 1685. Cabinets of this type were either of Oriental origin imported by the East India Company, or made in England and decorated in imitation by craftsmen and amateurs. The stands were made in England and are usually carved pine covered in gesso and then metal leaf.

orders of antiquity had become established. To a certain extent such designs began to influence interiors and artefacts also, as can be seen in the designs of Daniel Marot during the late seventeenth century and William Kent in the first part of the eighteenth century. However, it should be remembered that at this stage knowledge was limited to what the palaces and temples of the ancients looked like structurally, not how they were furnished. Until over half-way through the eighteenth century, our wonderful Palladian houses were for the most part decorated with items whose designs were born of European imagination, like baroque and rococo; Eastern influences as in our devotion to chinoiserie; and a resurgence of ecclesiastical patterns all mixed together to create the 'Gothic' style.

JAMES II (1685–88)

James II, second son of Charles I, and his court had no direct influence on furniture designs. Politically, he undid much of the good that Charles II had achieved and seemed to have learnt little from the fate of his father. Without direct influence, the development of design was for a short time left to the craftsmen. Chair backs were made higher, and tended to show a preference for baluster and vase turning, especially on the outside upright members. The seats became narrower, the spaces between the caning smaller and much finer. Otherwise, the basic shapes of furniture remained without any significant change and the industry might well have stagnated but for the impetus of craftsmen from the Continent. The Revocation of the Edict of Nantes in 1685 deprived the Huguenots (French Protestants) of all civil and religious rights and liberty and they were forced to flee the country to find sanctuary in Holland and the British Isles. The Huguenots were industrious and highly skilled. They brought to this country new standards of manufacture in woodwork and metalwork (see *Discovering Hallmarks on English Silver* by John Bly, Shire, 2000) as well as new techniques in weaving tapestries and cloth suitable for upholstery. Previously, only home needlework or fine brocades and velvets from Italy and, during the Commonwealth, leather, had been used to cover the seats and backs of chairs, but because of their formidable cost and, in the case of leather, comparative lack of comfort, only on a small scale. The government encouraged the weaving of fabric and, although the Upholders (later Upholsterers) Guild had been formed prior to 1460, it was not until the end of the seventeenth century that the upholsterer and use of fabric for decoration and comfort became integral parts of our furniture history.

WILLIAM AND MARY (1689–1702)

The next important development in furniture decoration came with the accession to the throne of William III and his wife, Mary II, daughter of James II. William was the son of William, Prince of Orange, and Mary, daughter of Charles I. After considerable discontent throughout England with the reign of James II, and following his flight to France and a brief interregnum from 11 December 1688 to 13 February 1689, William and Mary were invited to rule England jointly, the affairs of state being left to William alone. With a Dutch king interested in the arts, there was still more influence in our design from the Continent and, with a reigning queen, court and social behaviour again mimicked the latest in European culture. William III brought with him craftsmen skilled in the art of furniture manufacture and we can see evidence of Dutch influence in both the shape and decoration of much of the better quality household furniture of this post-Restoration period. The method of enhancing furniture with thin slices of wood fixed to the surface of the carcase or main body of an article was known as early as the second quarter of the seventeenth century but it really became popular in England during the 1690s. Now known as veneer, it was originally called 'faneer' because the slices were cut across the trunk or branch of the timber thus showing the 'fan', or medullar rays, of the timber rather than along the grain, a practice which became popular during the eighteenth century.

By this time, two complex forms of veneering – parquetry and marquetry – were used. Parquetry involves the use of regular-shaped pieces of veneer laid so as to form symmetrical or geometrical patterns. Marquetry is the application of a prepared pictured panel made of contrasting coloured veneers.

Walnut, now imported from France as well as Spain, and laburnum wood were the timbers essential for parquetry. Walnut was most used for moulded, cross-banded borders, while the branches of laburnum wood were cut at an angle, rather like cutting a loaf of French bread, to give oval shapes (oysters) and straight across to give round ones. Sometimes, the outer ring of sapwood was retained to enhance the oysters or rounds which were then arranged so as to form regular patterns on the

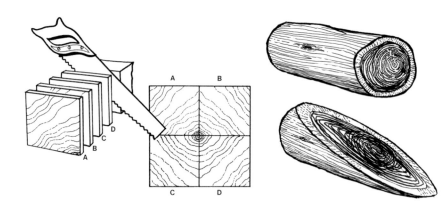

surface of the article to be decorated, much in the same manner as a parquet floor is created. Interspersing these patterns in circles were lines of box wood, about one-eighth of an inch square in section, known as stringing.

Marquetry, on the other hand, is a far more fanciful form of veneer decoration. There were two main styles in this period: floral, which used a great variety of woods to create differences in colour and texture, and seaweed or arabesque, which depended on just two colours laid in balanced scrolls. Floral marquetry, which is the earlier of the two, used designs incorporating foliate sprays, leaf scrolls, vines, flowers and birds usually within a framework of stringing and crossbanding of walnut or kingwood. For this, rosewood, sandalwood, box, acacia, holly, ebony, sycamore and occasionally ivory were used. Others were dyed to give additional colours and another skill was to scorch woods by dipping them in hot sand to give a shaded, three-dimensional effect to the pattern. Most other fruit woods were used, generally with a background of walnut. Arabesque marquetry, which was also sometimes used in conjunction with parquetry, used only two woods, usually box or holly, for the pattern on a walnut

Left and below:
A walnut lace or ruffle
box from 1680, inlaid
with marquetry flowers
and birds.

background. The patterns were of the most intricate scrollwork, demanding the highest possible degree of skill from the marquetry cutter and relying on the fineness of the work rather than an assortment of colour for its impact.

The earliest method of marquetry involved temporarily glueing together sheets of the various coloured veneers, with a layer of soft sugar paper between each, and clamping them together between rough timbers. The desired pattern would then be cut right through with a very fine-toothed saw. When the design had been fully cut, the woods were separated, using water and a thin-bladed knife to work away the paper between each slice. If, for example, four woods were used, there would now be four panels, each with a design which could be replaced by three other colours.

As walnut was the most popular background, not all the panels were used but were kept to be used in the event of breakages in subsequent repeats of the same design.

On seventeenth-century marquetry, the additional details of veins on leaves which appear to have been scribed into wood are, in fact, fine saw cuts. This makes it quite easy to date a piece accurately because the glue that rose through these cuts when the marquetry was applied caused tiny but distinct raised lines, whereas eighteenth-century classical

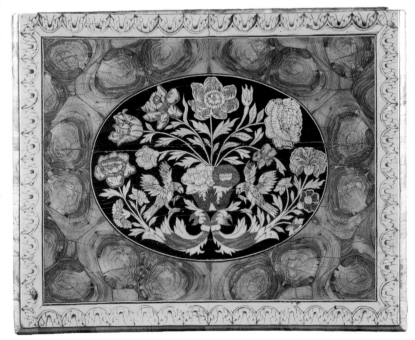

period marquetry had such additional detail scribed or etched on to the wood after the panel had been applied, giving a fine appearance but without the raised line effect.

Marquetry fell from favour during the Queen Anne period, but was revived in the second half of the eighteenth century and the practice of engraving it did not become popular until its revival. During the nineteenth century, when most marquetry was produced by machine, it became highly desirable once again.

Boulle or buhl work, a veneer created in the same way as traditional marquetry but using interlocking tortoiseshell (which is really turtle shell) and brass instead of differing woods, also became popular in Europe at the end of the seventeenth century. Red, deep yellow and green tortoiseshell could be created by varying the colour of the background surface to which the buhl was applied. Named after its creator, Andre Charles Boulle, it was most popular in France, and had gone out of fashion by the 1760s, but was revived and much used in England from the Regency period. The thin sheets of each material are glued together and the required design, generally of intricate scrolls and foliage, is cut through both diagonally. The glue is then melted and the designs and materials can be interchanged. The two alternatives of background or decoration material thus provided are known as 'buhl' or 'contre-buhl' and the furniture to be decorated in this way was often made in pairs to use both to best advantage.

Another type of veneering introduced during this period which remained popular well into the 1720s was known as 'quartering'. Quartering relied on the phenomenon that four slices of veneer cut from the same piece of wood either along or across the grain naturally have almost identical markings. Imagine a cube of timber from which four cuts of veneer have been taken. If, for example, the bottom left-hand corners are placed together when the four are laid out to form a large square, the pattern in the wood is repeated four times and joins itself at the edges. This method of decoration was employed all over the country, and some charming examples of attractive quartering on country-made furniture, the underneath or inside of which is often very poor quality, can still be found.

Cross-banding is yet another popular method of adorning fine furniture which became stylish at this time, and is a fine strip of veneer of variable width, usually about half an inch wide, cut so that the grain runs crossways rather than lengthways. Like quartering, it is cut from a cube of wood and sliced thinly. It is then used to 'frame' the edges of what would usually be otherwise plain pieces of furniture, often with the grain laid at right angles to the principal veneer or timber.

A refinement on this was the introduction of feathering, or herring-bone cross-banding. To achieve this effect, the first cut in the cube was made diagonally, and the two opposing strips cut from it laid side-by-side to form a mirror-image, each approximately 1/4 inch wide.

The raised mouldings on the drawer-fronts of earlier furniture were now being ousted by the veneers, and instead a much smaller moulding was placed on the carcase round the edge of the drawer opening. This took the form of a raised cross-banding of semi-circular and later semi-oval shape which was sometimes worked with a groove or 'reed' to give a double semi-circular section.

The 'walnut' period of English furniture ran from around 1660 to about 1730, and herring-bone banding was most popular during this time. However, fashion did not change overnight, and much furniture of the early mahogany period, which began in the 1730s, was made with considerable influence from the previous period.

With the continued demand for decorated furniture, whether lacquered, gilded or veneered, it was soon obvious that cheaper and softer woods than oak could be used for the construction of the carcase or main body of any piece, as well as for the ornately carved stands and frames. This is particularly true in England rather than the Continent. Pine and deal were used to a great extent, and the large flat surfaces required were formed by glueing planks of these woods side by side. Unfortunately, unless veneered on both sides, warping often occurred on open surfaces like doors and fold-over tops. Sometimes it is possible to see the construction of a carcase through the unevenness of the veneer surface when viewed obliquely against the light; this is also apparent on some pieces of English lacquer.

A major development in English furniture construction came during the late seventeenth century with the design and use of metal screws. By the 1720s, the use of this innovation had become standard practice in all the best cabinet workshops.

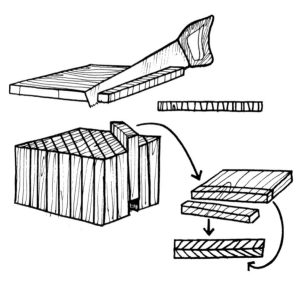

The method of cutting timber to produce (top) cross-banding and (bottom) herring-bone banding.

A William and Mary walnut side table from 1700 with oyster veneer. Note the X-shaped stretcher.

The tops of tables and chests, which had previously been fastened by pegging through, were now screwed on from underneath. Incisions with a rounded surface were made in the inside of the top rail to accommodate the screw, which went into the top at an angle. It was not until the nineteenth century that 'V' incisions for this purpose were made on English furniture.

THE INFLUENCE OF TEA

In 1700, the Joiners' Company, in a case against the 'Import of Manufactured Furniture and Cabinet Work', complained that, apart from the vast quantities of cabinets, chests, trunks, screens and chairs being unloaded at the Port of London by the East India merchants, over 6,500 lacquered tea tables had been imported within the previous four years. A tax of 15 per cent was subsequently put on all such merchandise, but the number shows just how popular tea drinking had become, and it is perhaps a reflection on the quality of the imported tea tables that apparently not one is known to have survived.

By this time, the East India Company merchants were importing large quantities of 'chaw', or tea, from China. Although it had been known in England since the early part of the seventeenth century, when it was first noted for its medicinal qualities, being thought a preventative against disease and a cure for hangover, tea did not affect our furniture industry until the late seventeenth century.

To begin with, the high price of the rare, black leaves imported in measures known as 'katis' (equal to slightly more than an avoirdupois pound) made it far too expensive for all but the wealthy to enjoy, but middle and poorer classes soon got the taste for it when they had access to the second or third brew in the servants'

A George II walnut silver table, the rectangular top with moulded edge above a frieze drawer and cabriole legs with pad feet

quarters. In 1679, the Duchess of Lauderdale is recorded as having a group of ladies to sample her chaw in the withdrawing room at Ham House where she entertained at what was probably the first ever 'tea party'. Here, and at every subsequent upper-class gathering, a great and lavish display of silver and oriental porcelain would have been presented on the tea table, and much protocol accorded to its use.

It is interesting to note that by the early 1720s, the specific time spent 'taking tea' – by now an elaborate excuse for gossip – had adopted the name of the table so that people attended a 'tea table' rather than a tea party, thus giving the piece of furniture an even more important position in the household inventory.

The first records of English tea tables describe them as being rectangular with a leg at each corner and a 'dished' or sunken top. They were equally decorated all round so that they could stand attractively in the middle of the room. During the reign of George I, this version was joined by the tripod base, centre column support tray-top tea table that in every conceivable shape, style and quality became one of the most produced pieces of English furniture in history. The earliest and commonest form of this type of table has a plain circular top supported by a turned and tapering column, similar in shape to, and thereby given the name of, a 'gun barrel' stem. This is fixed at the base to a triform block with concave sides, each end of which houses one of the three curved legs.

Generally speaking, by the 1750s the triform block had been made redundant by the new fashion for fixing the legs straight into the bottom end of the column, each with a large full-length dovetail joint – the column always housing the dovetail on

Below left:
A fine mid eighteenth-century tripod tea table, the legs and rim to the top carved in the rococo manner while the stem is formed as an architectural column.

Below:
An eighteenth-century tripod-base tea table, with tilting top. The claw and ball foot was a popular style, and was supposed to represent the sacred pearl of wisdom clasped by the dragon's claw.

A George II mahogany tea table from 1750 with tripod legs. The birdcage just visible beneath the gallery top allowed the table to revolve as well as tip. Note the acanthus carved knees and lion's paw feet.

the leg. Sometimes these three joints were further secured by a simple triform piece of metal attached by screws across the joints – a sort of belt-and-braces measure of quality. By this time a baluster shape column had also become popular, soon followed by a cup shape which was usually turned with lobing in a spiral pattern. The top of the table, which might be rectangular, straight sided or curved, as well as circular, may or may not have been 'dished', or have some sort of applied gallery around the edge supported by a fretwork or spindles. (The 'baluster' or double-curved shape of each turned spindle followed the outline of baluster supports for the stairways and galleries of Palladian houses and is also the basic design for contemporary coffee pots, hot water jugs, tankards and mugs.) These were expensive and top-of-the-range tables, but whether fancy or plain, the tops were always made to tip or tilt to the vertical position enabling the table to be put aside when not in use. This tilting was achieved by extending two corners of the square block which was fixed to the top of the column. These extensions, usually one inch long, were shaped round to fit precisely into holes bored into the insides of the two bearers, which were secured by screws to the underside of the top.

A further sophistication of this was the 'birdcage' fitment, which allowed the top to be rotated as well as tilted. This involved the use of two blocks acting as the hub of a wheel with the column as the axle.

In addition, the fold-over-top card table could obviously be used to present and serve tea, and by the 1730s it became common practice to make a pair, one with the inner surface of polished wood rather than covered with cloth or needlework, thus providing one for tea and one for gaming. These tables followed precisely the latest changes in design for the next hundred years.

Another requirement of the cabinet-maker soon grew out of the demand for small decorative boxes to contain the tea. To begin with, katis (or 'caddies') were fitted into chests for transportation and, as their popularity grew, first the chest and then the kati boxes became decorated. The katis were usually of tin and either lightly engraved in the chinoiserie manner, or japanned. The early container chests had hinged lids and were usually covered with fine morocco leather and embellished with silver and/or gilt metal hinges, corners and locks.

During the eighteenth century, these small tea chests of single, double or triple compartments were made of all manner of materials by all manner of people in large workshops and cottages alike. Towards the end of the eighteenth century, the

Left:
A mid-eighteenth-century mahogany lowboy, the moulded edge of broken serpentine outline above a frieze drawer flanked by two short drawers on lappet carved cabriole legs and pad feet.

Below:
A George III mahogany and kingwood toilet mirror showing the classic vase shape so popular after the 1770s.

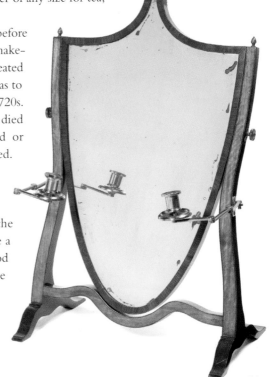

word 'caddy' was generally adopted as meaning a container of any size for tea, now being drunk by all and sundry.

There were other major changes in domestic furniture before the end of the seventeenth century. A growing use of make-up by both sexes (to camouflage the ravages of the pox) created a demand for the small, single-drawer side table which was to evolve into the dressing or toilet table, or 'lowboy' of the 1720s. It is after the Restoration period, when people actually died from applying too much make-up with a white lead or mercury base, that toilet tables are specifically mentioned. Their design is similar to that of the side table until the 1720s, except that the single shallow drawer was narrower and flanked by a deep drawer at each end, accommodated in a more deeply shaped frieze. From the beginning of the eighteenth century, it was usual to have a dressing table made with a matching toilet mirror that stood on the top. This was a simply framed mirror plate connected to two upright supports by two swivel screws, and usually with a box-type base below containing one or two rows of small drawers.

Chapter Three

QUEEN ANNE AND GEORGIAN

QUEEN ANNE, 1702–14

ON THE DEATH of William III in 1702, Anne, then aged 37 and second daughter of James II, succeeded to the throne. She was a thoroughly good woman – gentle, amiable and kind. Hers was an age of great men of science, literature and politics, and while John Churchill, Duke of Marlborough led England in war against France, his wife, Sarah Jennings was, for most of the reign, the Queen's best and most influential friend. The years 1706–7 saw the final Union of England and Scotland, and in the history of English furniture there was also unity; the beginnings of a combination of comfort and elegance in general middle-class articles. In terms of design, though, looking back to the exuberance of the late seventeenth century and forward to the mayhem to come, Queen Anne furniture can be seen as the calm between two storms.

Comfort became, for the first time, an important ingredient in design. The backs of chairs, for example, were shaped in solid wood to fit the body of the sitter, wonderful even today for sufferers of a bad back. The large, centre splat of stylised vase shape was surrounded by a curved frame, and the seat continued this shape by ballooning out towards the front. Fully upholstered wing armchairs were popular, with deep cushions in the seats, short curved legs at the front and splay legs at the back. For construction, English as well as imported walnut was now used, and a taste for less ornate decoration accentuated the importance of good design and careful choice of timber. One popular carved motif of the period was the scallop shell, which was used to decorate the friezes and front rails, and to cap the knees of the curved legs on all types of furniture. The form of the curved leg during the Queen Anne period is now called 'cabriole'. This had developed from the Flemish moulded curve terminating in either the Braganza foot or an animal's paw. *Cabriole* was a French dancing term meaning a bound or leap, hence its initial use in describing a furniture leg that terminated in a cloven-hoofed foot. This foot remained a popular motif in Europe, while England adopted the curved leg, preferring to add a 'claw and ball' foot – a further illustration of a love of Oriental mythology, as it was said to represent the sacred pearl of wisdom clasped by the dragon's claw. As the curve of the knee became simplified during the early eighteenth century, the leg often ended in a simple pad foot, particularly, but not exclusively, in the provinces.

By this time, the entire interior arrangements of houses had begun to change. The introduction of large, tall windows, imposing fireplaces and doorways required furniture of the same proportions to achieve a balanced effect. Console or pier tables

Opposite:
The lacquer closet at Beningborough Hall, North Yorkshire. Oriental lacquer fascinated the wealthy people of northern Europe; so much so that in addition to importing oriental pieces, we sent our native furniture to the East to be lacquered. Here we see an oriental cabinet and two English chairs, some examples of which were even decorated with English faux lacquer in competition with the foreign imports.
(Country Life Picture Library)

with tall mirrors (pier glasses) made their debut although they did not become truly fashionable until the 1720s when their use was much encouraged by the designs of William Kent and the improvements in the production of large plates of glass. Case furniture became taller and narrower in rooms other than the library. A typical example of this new development was the bureau-cabinet, the earliest examples of which were made in three parts. The top part of an escritoire with its deeply sloping front enclosing several small drawers and compartments, was placed on a low chest of drawers base instead of an open stand. The horizontal top part of the escritoire bore a double door cupboard with either solid wood or mirror glass panels and these were surmounted by a shaped cornice which at this time could be single, double dome or flat. To ensure that the cupboard sat securely on the escritoire base,

Above:
A Queen Anne walnut open armchair from 1710, with show-wood frame and a shaped wishbone stretcher.

Above right:
A George I walnut chair with carved and shaped back splat. The cabriole legs are carved with shells to the knee, and have leaf scroll brackets and claw and ball feet. Stretcher rails are rarely found on chairs of this pattern but reappear after the 1750s.

a substantial moulding was placed around the edge of the escritoire. A similar moulding was placed round the chest/escritoire joint and large metal carrying handles were often fixed on the sides of all three pieces. The feet would be a turned bun shape or later a plain bracket. Some bureaux and bureau-cabinets of this period have the base constructed with a row of small drawers placed one

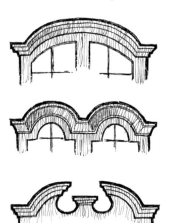

Bottom left:
Three examples of cornice shapes that were fashionable during the first quarter of the eighteenth century.

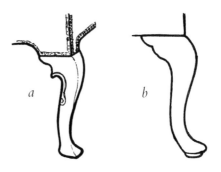

Above: The curved leg, introduced and becoming popular in England during the early eighteenth century. The square section foot (a) preceded the round pad foot (b) but survived alongside it until 1725.

Left: A George I walnut and crossbanded kneehole desk with ogee bracket feet. One long drawer sits above two sets of three smaller drawers, 1720.

Opposite bottom right: A George I walnut crossbanded and featherbanded bureau-cabinet with ogee moulded shaped cornice. Just beneath the mirror door panels are candle slides. 1720.

Right: An early George I walnut crossbanded and featherbanded chest on a stand, or tallboy. This was the earlier style of tallboy, with a chest on top of a lowboy-style base, 1715.

above another on each side of a recessed compartment to accommodate the knees of the writer. This same construction was used for some types of knee-hole dressing tables and the flat-top knee-hole writing desk. The recessed compartment soon disappeared from the bureau, however, for the open lid or 'fall' provided ample space for knees, making the recess a needless waste of drawer space. Until the 1720s, most walnut period bureaux have three long drawers below a deep top rail, sometimes decorated to simulate a drawer front. The space behind this dummy drawer was accessible only by opening the fall, which could be locked. Inside, a portion of the writing surface slid back underneath the small drawers and compartments, revealing a secret compartment known as a 'well'. This characteristic disappeared during the 1730s and the space was filled with a proper drawer accessible from the front when the bureau fall was closed, just like the other drawers.

The tallboy was another innovation of the early 1700s. This described a chest of drawers set upon a base, similar in appearance to, but larger than, the lowboy. By the 1720s, this lower part was replaced by a chest of three or four long drawers and the 'chest-on-chest' or tallboy became an established household item.

Above:
A George I walnut-framed wing armchair with cabriole shell, bellflower legs and pad feet.

Right:
A George I walnut dining chair in the manner of Giles Grendey, a cabinet and chair-maker of the time who ran a major export business from London. This chair has a paper scroll top-rail, cabriole legs with shell carved knees and claw and ball feet, 1730.

Being so useful, they were popular in bachelor apartments and often had a brushing slide – a shelf that pulled out from above the top drawer in the lower part – on which linen and clothing could be spread out and made fresh, and occasionally they were fitted with secretaire writing drawers. A word of warning here: these secretaire fitments were also added later to enhance the value.

The Queen Anne style prevailed well into the 1720s, as if English cabinet-makers needed a break to settle down and prepare themselves for the expansive times ahead when the production of fine furniture would elevate some from craftsman status to high society, making them extremely wealthy in the process.

GEORGE I, 1714–27

Queen Anne's only surviving child died in 1701. In order to ensure the succession of a Protestant monarch, the crown was to devolve upon Sophia, Electress of Hanover, granddaughter of James II. However, she died shortly before Anne, so her son George was proclaimed king in 1714, and was crowned at Westminster later that year. He was the first sovereign of the House of Hanover. Apart from a Jacobite rising in 1715, and the well-known financial 'South Sea Bubble', the reign of George I was peaceful.

Possibly through his lack of interest in design and fashions (and his preference for Hanover), coupled with the increase in the number of people able to afford fine houses and furnishings, the leading styles from the early years of George I to about 1800 are generally recognised by the name of the style or its designer, as well as the name of the reigning monarch. For example, the term 'rococo' is used as well as George II, and Hepplewhite or Adam as well as George III.

From 1710 to 1720, a combination of the best features of the previous fifteen years produced a subtle, functional and attractive style of

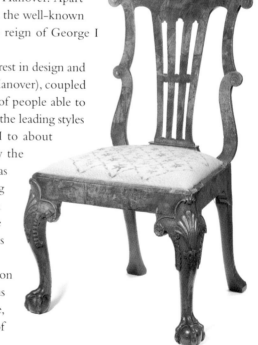

furniture. The outlines formed the basis for many of the elaborate designs of the 1740s and 1750s, and can often be discerned under the extravagant decoration of the rococo period.

By 1720, the craft of furniture making had become a complex industry employing joiners, turners, carvers, gilders, clock and barometer makers, mirror-glass makers, fine metal workers and upholsterers. In London and other major cities, each branch of the industry became a specialised but integral part in an ever-expanding trade. The construction of British furniture took pride of place as the finest in the world, matching even that made for the French court, whence came the basis for many of our own designs in the baroque and rococo manner. At this time, most of the furniture being made in England fell into one of four categories. There were the finest pieces, made to the most up-to-date designs by appointed craftsmen for royal and aristocratic households, which were the first to display any new style or decorative motif. Then there was the furniture made in London and larger towns throughout the country for the minor aristocracy, rich merchants and country squires, always of the best quality, but slightly less flamboyant. The mass of middle-class mahogany furniture was made for the moderately wealthy families. The proportions of this furniture are invariably faultless, and even country-made pieces have great charm because the basic designs of the period lent themselves to simple, unadorned production – characterful, curvilinear, yet plain – and always pleasing to the eye. Finally there was the country or cottage furniture made by retained joiners on the large estates for the homes of the tenants. Such 'country' furniture was also made by village carpenters for local houses. For the most part it is the middle-class furniture which, because of the sheer quantity, forms the bulk of what is today recognised as eighteenth-century antique furniture.

The five orders of Classical architecture, from left to right: Doric, Composite, Tuscan, Ionic, Corinthian. Great importance was attached to a detailed knowledge of Classical architecture in general, and these orders in particular, by designers and craftsmen during the eighteenth century, and variations are shown in design books of the period. Those illustrated in Chippendale's Director are not fluted, but the basic proportions must remain as the original. Apart from the decoration to base, cap and entablature, each has a specified size, e.g. Corinthian and Composite are ten diameters high, Ionic nine diameters high, Doric eight and Tuscan seven.

It is important to remember that at this time, while the proportions of grand houses were based on the noble orders of ancient architecture, established in Greek and Roman antiquity, no one knew how the occupants furnished their homes. Designers drew, therefore, on three main sources for decorative inspiration: our sacred and secular past, depicted by 'Gothic'; the mythical east as portrayed by chinoiserie, and the sheer imaginative romance and whimsy delineated in the forms of baroque and rococo. Palladian style related mainly to architecture and was restricted, naturally, to fitments like library bookcases and larger pieces such as cabinets and desks.

By the 1730s, the timber most used for the two finest classes of furniture was mahogany and, to a lessening degree, walnut. Mahogany was used for some time in

An early eighteenth-century baroque-style marble-topped side table in the ponderous manner of William Kent. The heavy carving and eagle subject is typically baroque.

the solid rather than being cut for veneer, for it lent itself admirably to the skills of a good carver and was a considerable encouragement to the growing taste for flamboyant decoration in the Palladian, baroque, rococo, Chinese and Gothic patterns, which were to remain 'high style' until the late 1760s.

ROCOCO AND BAROQUE

The word 'baroque', applied to furniture, meant any whimsical, idealistic, asymmetrical design of ponderous proportions. Heavy carved scrolls, eagles with spread wings, masks, torsos, *amorini* (cherubs), huge sea shells and other fantastic motifs accentuated with gilding and enriched with fine brocades and velvets were the fashion in France and Italy during the last half of the seventeenth century and early eighteenth century, and gained an important but limited appeal in England, particularly after the exclusive popularity of Daniel Marot and William Kent. Magnificence without elegance might be a suitable summary.

The rococo style originated in France, where Pierre Lepautre (*c.*1700), Claude Audran (1658–1734), Nicholas Pineau (1684–1754) and later, J. A. Meissonnier (1696–1750) were among the leading protagonists. The world 'rococo' comes from the French word *rocaille*, meaning 'rockwork', and in England it is used to describe a really refined simplification of baroque, with rocks, garlands and festoons of floral motifs used for both the background and the highlight of the decoration. The rococo style continued in England during the early 1740s and remained the predominant fashion for nearly ten years.

A George III gilt wood mirror with carved rococo 'C' scrolls and fronded leaves, 1765.

PALLADIAN

Named after the Italian architect Andrea Palladio (1508–80), who based his work on the styles of ancient Rome, the Palladian style with its clean and elegant lines was promoted vigorously by Inigo Jones (1573–1652). As chief architect to Charles I, Jones made the distinctive style of classical columns, arches and pediments familiar on the stately homes and public buildings of the period such as the Queen's House, Greenwich. The style continued as an undercurrent or alternative to the chaotic rococo and baroque until the mid-eighteenth century, when it became a natural adjunct to the 'Adam' classical and neo-classical movements.

GOTHIC

Eighteenth-century Gothic taste took as its theme medieval styles, following either patterns reminiscent of church and cathedral design or of the ancient castle and its interior. The legs of pot stands, night cupboards (commodes), tables and chairs etc. might be formed as 'cluster columns'. Open fret-cut corner brackets and 'crocketed' chair backs had simulated church window shapes as their basis, and the cornices and friezes of cabinets were often embattled. This style of Gothic had been in evidence since the early 1720s, but between 1740 and 1765 reached its peak, considerably encouraged by the popularity of Horace Walpole's extraordinary mansion, Strawberry Hill at Twickenham. So famous was this house that its name became synonymous with the style, and visitors from the Continent made the pilgrimage to see it, for there are no records of a similar style in Europe. Ironically, at its height, through the romantic designs of Batty Langley, Thomas Chippendale and several other contemporaries, Gothic taste became so fanciful that it bore little, if any, relationship to its origins. The Gothic style that appeared again during the nineteenth century showed a much more realistic appreciation of true medieval design, especially in George Smith's *Household Furniture* published in 1808.

George IV Gothic revival oak dining chairs showing the ecclesiastical taste, which influenced Victorian design for much of the nineteenth century.

SECOND CHINOISERIE

Although the practice of japanning furniture had continued since its introduction during the latter part of the seventeenth century, the taste for imported Oriental furniture declined during the early part of the eighteenth century, to be replaced by its more colourful English counterpart. During the early 1740s, however, a revival of all chinoiserie was encouraged by the wide circulation of books on foreign travel. The two most important of these were the magnificent work on China by the Frenchman J. B. du Halde and *Designs of Chinese Buildings* by Sir William Chambers. The English version of the former was published in weekly instalments during 1742 and, like Chambers' book published in 1757, showed mirrors, frames, torchères, cabinets, bookcases, beds, dressing tables and other household items which were all European pieces, not Chinese, enriched with Chinese decoration. So mid-eighteenth-century chinoiserie was more Anglo-Chinese than the earlier seventeenth-century version.

One of the finest examples of this is to be found at Claydon House, Buckinghamshire. Here, pagodas, ho-ho birds, dragons and cracked-ice fencing sit with tea-drinking, moustachioed mandarins amid decaying ancient orders, cluster columns and asymmetrical alcoves.

The Chinese Room from Claydon House in Buckinghamshire, carved by Luke Lightfoot. This is the epitome of the mid-eighteenth-century Chinoiserie style in England which often incorporated elements of high rococo and even some gothic. Genuine Chinese designs were melded with European imagination to create a fantastical assembly. (Claydon House/John Bethell/The Bridgeman Art Library)

WASHING STANDS AND NIGHT TABLES

In 1724, Messrs Gumley and Moore recorded making three tables of mahogany, one 'supping' and the other two 'desart'. This is not only one of the earliest references to mahogany in the manufacture of furniture, but it also gives an indication of the now numerous and diverse uses for which articles of furniture were being made. During the 1740s and 1750s, several items of furniture first began to appear in quantity. Two such pieces were washing stands and night tables, which by the 1760s had become standard equipment for the bedrooms of every well-appointed house. The earliest types of washing stands are sometimes called wig stands, and night tables are referred to as pot-cupboards, or, the larger type, commodes.

The manufacture and use of soap had been known in England since the fourteenth century, but it was not until the latter half of the seventeenth century that a full cleansing toilet became part of a daily routine, and even then only for a minority of the population. The introduction during this period of brushes for cleaning teeth and the beginning of an interest in personal cleanliness suggests that the small occasional table in the bedroom would have had its single drawer full of washing requisites as well as cosmetic preparations. In addition, from around 1685 until the early part of the nineteenth century, it was fashionable for gentlemen to shave, and from 1720 it was proper to wear a powdered wig. Thus, social behaviour added two more reasons for further development in the furniture industry. Despite the earlier demand there are to date no known authentic examples of stands or tables made specifically to hold jugs and washing bowls prior to the 1740s, when two main types were being made. One has a folding top which encloses the bowl and soap compartments; the other is of triform shape and quite open. It has a circular ring for the bowl supported by three generally curved uprights above one or two triangular drawers; these were on three similar supports terminating on a triangular platform which was usually turned or dished to accommodate a pitcher or small bowl, and the whole thing was raised from the floor by three curved legs. As the soap was produced in round lumps, and was known as a 'wash ball', a small turned spherical cup and cover was often fixed in the centre of the platform above the drawer(s) as the soap box. When this was made detachable, a hole was bored in the base of the cup, which then fitted on to a peg fixed to the platform. This type of stand is commonly known today as a wig stand, the theory being that the wig was put on its block, placed in the bowl and then powdered; when not in use the block stood on the bottom platform.

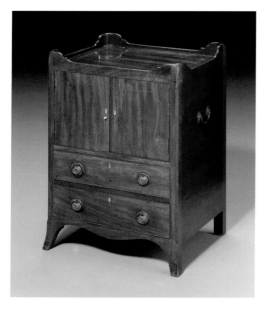

During the second quarter of the eighteenth century, the pot-cupboard, night table, and commodious armchair were introduced as a development from the close stool. This type of enclosed chamber pot and seat had been used in large houses and castles since the latter part of the fifteenth century, and during the seventeenth century had become disguised as small trunks and chests. During the first half of the eighteenth century they were usually in the shape of a lift-top box with side carrying handles and on four plain bracket feet, either of walnut or (later) mahogany. Toward the middle of the century close stools were of two main types. One was a small cupboard supported on four tall legs; the other was a larger cupboard with a deep drawer below, of which the front two legs were split and the drawer housing the chamber pot could be pulled out to provide a seat. The commode chair was a large, open-frame chair with a loose upholstered seat frame covering the pot which was concealed from the front and sides by a deep shaped rail. One reason that for many years night tables have been referred to in England as commodes was that most of the finest examples of the later eighteenth century were made to look like small chests or cupboards for which the French name was *commode*. This word essentially describes a low chest with drawers, which unlike the English type of chest of drawers is wider in relation to its height, and, being made only for the finer houses, was always the object of the most elaborate or fashionable decoration. After the middle of the century, the serpentine and bombe shapes were much used for the construction of commodes in the French taste, and two doors often replaced the drawers to form a cupboard. The highest degree of skill and accuracy was needed to make a commode and those that can be seen in museums and country houses today afford us a close look at the work of many of the leading cabinet-makers and designers of the eighteenth century. When describing a fine eighteenth century chest as a commode, stress or accent is on the first syllable – *com*mode; an English night table has the stress on the last syllable – com*mode*.

Above left:
An English mahogany night table commode c. 1770. Late eighteenth-century examples often incorporated a tambour shutter rather than solid panel top doors. This is a series of thin strips of wood glued to canvas, which can be pushed back into the sides of the cupboard compartment.

Above:
A George III satinwood and kingwood crossbanded gentleman's dressing table, attributed to Seddon, Sons & Shackleton.

CHEST FURNITURE

From the 1740s, the basic concept of chest furniture did not change. The tallboy with a chest of two short and three long drawers on a high cabriole leg stand was being replaced by the mid-1730s by one with the base part made of another chest of usually four long drawers on ogee or plain bracket feet, and the top cresting became flat. The bureau-bookcases and cabinets, with either blind (solid wood) or glazed doors to the upper half had similar feet, but the top cresting remained an important feature on those of better quality until the 1790s. As a general guide – not to be taken as a definite rule – until around 1750 these crestings were architectural and most later ones became deeply curved in what is known as a swan-neck cornice and often incorporated pierced fret cutting in the recessed panels. This type had been used for mirror frame crestings since around 1730. The blind doors were panelled and framed either in straight rectangular form or shaped, the latter being described as a fielded panel. The glazed doors progressed quite quickly from plain rectangular

A George III mahogany chest-on-chest, or tallboy from 1770. In the manner of Thomas Chippendale, this tallboy has a Greek key cornice, ogee bracket feet, and original swing handles.

frames of six, eight or ten panes of glass with substantial moulding, to a much finer tracery effect with delicate 'astragal' mouldings separating the glass. From 1760 on, glazed doors for furniture attained an unsurpassed quality of design and construction, and as such could be made in the chinoiserie, Gothic and Classical patterns as well as the more usual geometric type. Of the latter, those having thirteen or fifteen separate panes of glass in each door are regarded as being of better quality. One significant change during the 1730s in the appearance of chest furniture was the shape of the drawer fronts. Following the practice during the early walnut period of placing a single reeded moulding on to the carcase of the chest round the drawer opening, the moulding disappeared, and the drawer front was made to overhang approximately 1/4 inch all round the drawer. This was formed with a fractional step and a quarter circle section. In many cases, the overhang was on the bottom and side edges only, a simulated moulding being worked on to the top edge, thus giving the appearance of shallower drawers and dispensing with the nuisance of the top lip which could snag or catch when the drawer was used. This method of drawer construction continued well into the 1730s and was used on mahogany and Virginian walnut chests of the period. However, by this time a new construction had been introduced, the application of a 'cock bead'. The earliest known examples of this date from around 1730; therefore it can be safely assumed that a piece with cock-beaded drawer fronts will have been made after 1735, allowing a few years for the idea to spread and be accepted as an improvement. After this development, the drawer front became flush with the carcase and receded fully into the opening. It was marked, however, by a thin semi-circular moulding which protruded up to one eighth of an inch all round the drawer. This can best be described as the extended edge of a frame of veneer, and its application formed the final phase of the construction of the drawer. It proved to be completely satisfactory, and the cock bead remained the standard finish for drawers of good-quality furniture throughout the remainder of the eighteenth century. A poor substitute often found on cheaper articles is a line simply gouged out to simulate a cock bead, but this is easily discernible and is the mark of at best a country-made piece.

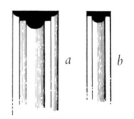

Astragal mouldings. Used correctly, the term 'astragal' describes a semi-circular moulding or bead in architecture, but it has for many years been applied to the glazing bars on English cabinet furniture. The types shown are (a) first half of the eighteenth century, becoming finer; (b) second half of the eighteenth century.

Below left:
A mahogany serpentine chest showing an Adam influence in the choice of handles.

Below:
The moulding of the overhanging drawer front, which became worked into the top edge of the drawer front prior to around 1735, when the cock-bead became more popular.

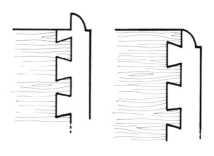

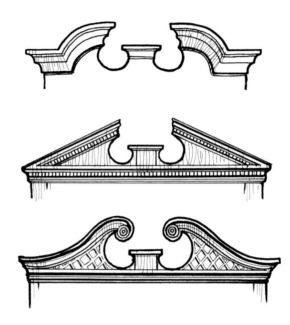

Above: The development of bookcase and cabinet cornices.
(a) 1700–30.
(b) 1725–70, the architectural broken pediment.
(c) 1765–90, the swan-neck cornice shown here with open fret carving in the recessed panels. This type was popular for the crestings of fine mirrors as early as c. 1730.

Above: A George III mahogany and satinwood banded secretaire in the manner of Mordecai Kitching of Hull, c. 1800.

Right: A George III mahogany bow-front sideboard, with arched apron and turned tapering legs, 1810.

DINING FURNITURE

Prior to the middle of the eighteenth century, the average dining room contained virtually no cupboard spaces. The napery was brought in by the servants, and until the early eighteenth century it was normal for people to retain their own cutlery, travelling with the three utensils – knife, spoon and recently introduced fork – in a fitted case. By about 1720 it became fashionable for wealthy families to have sets of cutlery, which were kept in cutlery or 'knife' boxes, made for the benefit of guests as well as themselves. The all-encompassing canteen as we know it did not appear until the early nineteenth century. The display of wealth in the form of jugs, basins, platters, chargers and dishes of silver, gold or gold plate remained on display on one of the 'board' tables. These followed the pattern of the other side, pier or console tables in the house and often had a marble top. In average, middle-class households, any suitable table was used. By the 1760s, however, serving tables flanked by urns on pedestal cupboards were introduced, and by the 1780s these had been incorporated into one piece of furniture, the sideboard. This development coincided with the introduction of a host of items such as plate carriers, dumb waiters, wine coolers, cheese coasters, bottle sliders and cellarets – all previously little known and therefore rare before the 1750s.

DINING TABLES

During the Restoration period it had become fashionable to set aside a separate room for eating, and by the early eighteenth century most houses built in contemporary style had a proper dining room. It is strange, therefore, that little importance seems to have been attached to the designs of dining tables until the second half of the eighteenth century. Before then, particularly for family meals, a simple drop-leaf table was used; sometimes two or three were joined together to seat a larger number of people. In design, they follow a natural progression from the gate-leg table, which remained popular until the early 1720s. By the 1730s, the gate

A Regency mahogany extended table in the manner of Gillows of Lancaster.

Above left and right: A Sheraton period Pembroke table, the top inlaid with oval and rectangular panels, standing on square taper legs.

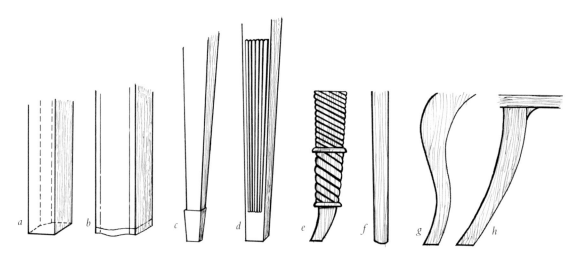

The development of chair legs from 1750 to 1820.
(a) The straight untapered leg with the inside corner chamfered. Often the ground for blind fret work in the Chinese or Gothic manner, or left plain for country furniture, 1750–65. (b) The straight moulded front leg 1760–90. (c) The plain taper leg terminating in spade foot, from around 1775. By 1800 the spade foot had become less popular and the taper leg was decorated with cross-banding and/or stringing. During the early

Regency period reeding (d) became popular and is considered more typical of the period than fluting, although both are used. Reeding is convex, fluting is concave. (e) Fine and heavy spiral turning and a circular section splay foot, early 1800s.
(f) and (g) The return of the elongated ogee curved leg with semi-circular moulding to the front, and straight sides, first quarter of the nineteenth century. (h) The Grecian curved or sabre leg, first quarter of the nineteenth century.

the 1760s, wherein square-sectioned legs were tapered, to be revived shortly afterwards in a modified version commonly attributed to George Hepplewhite, where the front facing sides were moulded. This is truer of the legs on chairs and larger tables, for the smaller tripod-base tea table retained the cabriole-type curved leg until much later in the century.

A Chippendale period tripod table of finest quality would have considerable carving on the base and a dished top with probably a shaped rim, similar to the border of a good 1750 period silver salver. In fact, the effect was intended to simulate a tray on a stand, which, being pivoted on the block under the top, could be tilted upright to stand against the wall when not in use. The vast majority of tripod tables made in the provinces (of which there were many thousands) were, of course, quite plain, while genuine eighteenth-century dished-top and carved tripod tables were rare. Unfortunately for today's collector, furniture of this latter type was extremely popular during the early twentieth century and a great many shapely but plain pieces entered the workshops of skilled fakers to reappear carved and dished, so again – beware! The 'birdcage' under the table top enabled the table to revolve as well as tip up but, although it is accepted as a mark of quality, a table without a 'birdcage' is not necessarily inferior.

OTHER DINING ROOM FURNITURE

Dumb-waiters were, as their name suggests, introduced to hold food and cutlery during and after a meal when the servants had been dismissed and when, thanks to the mellowing effects of good food and fine wines, the conversation might become indiscreet. A dumb-waiter is a two-, three- or four-tiered stand on a tripod base with castors. Each tier was formed as a circular revolving tray, graduated in size and supported on a central column. The best examples follow the contemporary designs of decoration from the 1740s onwards for, although they are mentioned in earlier times, they were not generally popular until after this date. On good quality examples the trays are dished and a thin, unwarped tray shows the maker's careful choice of fine timber. From the lower tray up, each column section should unscrew, making the replacement of a broken tray a simple procedure.

The quality and colour of the timber will usually show if this has occurred recently. During the latter part of the eighteenth century, and particularly during the Regency period, the bases of dumb-waiters often incorporated complicated sections with drawers and compartments and followed the classical, and later heavier styles.

There may be confusion between a dumb-waiter and a what-not. The reason is that the nineteenth-century designs for both were often similar. The term 'what-not' usually describes a set of rectangular trays, one above another with the supports at the outer edges and often incorporating one or two drawers in the base. Following its introduction during the last fifteen years of the eighteenth century the what-not was made in various sizes and to all manner of designs.

Even more confusion has arisen over the definitions of wine coolers and cellarets. Both were made to hold bottles of wine, and the confusion may well have occurred because during the latter part of the eighteenth century the cellaret was often constructed to serve as both holder and cooler. The earliest known wooden wine coolers or cisterns are *c.* 1730 and are formed as long, open basins lined with lead. They contained ice or very cold water and held the bottles of wines to be served during a meal. After *c.*1750, the most popular type was constructed in the same way as a barrel, the sides being straight and sometimes tapering, shaped oval or round and hooped with bands of brass. A tap was inserted at the base and the whole thing was made either to fit into a four-legged stand or to rest on a sideboard pedestal. In the Regency period they were mostly floor-standing on four feet carved as lions' paws.

Cellarets are lidded boxes of oval, round, hexagonal, octagonal or square shape. The interiors are divided into compartments

Left:
A George III mahogany two-tier dumb waiter on tripod base with plain curved legs and pad feet, 1765. From the middle of the eighteenth century dumb-waiters developed in line with other tripod base occasional furniture, having three, four and even five tiers. Towards the end of the century these were sometimes made to drop down like the leaves of a Pembroke table, being supported by a revolving bar.

Right:
A George III mahogany cellaret, attributed to Gillows of Lancaster.

to take a certain number of bottles and, being fitted with a lock and key, they were initially intended to hold a small stock of wine in the dining room at all times. Cellarets came into general use during the 1760s and were also lead-lined, free-standing on feet with castors, and were used extensively until the 1780s when a cellaret drawer was first fitted into one end of the sideboard. The larger and more important types of cellaret continued to be made until the mid-Regency period, but more often with a tap in the base and were therefore used as coolers as well as containers. The ice used was frozen water gathered from lakes or pools in winter and stored in deep pits or ice houses.

Above left:
A George III wine cooler with lion mask and ring handle.

Above:
A pair of George IV satinwood étagères with three-quarter pierced brass galleries. The étagère is a light piece of furniture, mainly made in France, and very similar to the English what-not.

Left: A Regency carved mahogany cellaret of sarcophagus type, which became popular after the turn of the eighteenth to nineteenth century.

CANTERBURYS AND DAVENPORTS

Small stands for containing specific items were numerous, often being individually commissioned and later gaining general popularity. One such is the Canterbury. According to Thomas Sheraton, the Canterbury is either an open, box-like stand, partitioned to take music, or a shaped stand on tall legs to hold plates and cutlery. The latter is generally referred to today as a plate stand, but the original name for both types is purported to have derived from the Primate of all England who first ordered the manufacture of such pieces. Another new model dates from the latter part of the eighteenth century and is first recorded as being made by Messrs Gillow of Lancaster for a Captain Davenport. Davenports became popular during the Regency period and, following contemporary designs, were made throughout the nineteenth century. The later types lost the sliding top which formed the knee space and were constructed more like school desks, with the sides supported on turned or scroll columns. The most expensive type had a curved or 'piano' top incorporating a counterbalanced rising section for stationery.

The sofa table was another writing table which, having been introduced during the last quarter of the eighteenth century, became extremely popular at the beginning of the nineteenth. This is a long version of the Pembroke table with the two leaves at the narrow sides of the top hinged to form drop ends. The underframe of the top contains two or four shallow drawers, and is supported by a pillar at each end with two splay feet terminating in brass cap castors. The original purpose of this kind of table was to provide a writing surface which could be drawn over the end of the sofa, hence the name. This is why the earlier examples have the strengthening rail high off the ground or arched in a suitable manner. Very soon, however, the rail was lowered and, as it was now visible, decorated to match the rest of the table. Despite the fact that this obviated its original use, the name remained for tables of this style. During the Regency period, sofa tables with a centre column, shaped platform and curved legs became more fashionable and this type, in gradually increasing degrees of heavy design, continued to enjoy popularity until the 1840s.

By the 1760s, most middle-class houses had a separate withdrawing room, dining room, hall, reception room and, in some cases, a library. Each of these rooms was elegantly furnished with a host of smaller, occasional furniture. Apart from card tables, breakfast, tea and supper tables, there were Pembrokes and ladies' writing tables in reception rooms; dining rooms boasted sets of chairs and a dining table, a dumb-waiter, wine cooler, cellaret, serving table, plate-warmer, cutlery boxes and probably a large, leather draught screen. The hall contained at least one console table with a pier glass over, hall chairs, a pair of torchères and a large centre table. In the library, one would expect to find a drum-top table, library steps, reading chairs and a pair of celestial and terrestrial

An early Victorian satinwood three-division Canterbury in the manner of John C. Louden, with drawer below. This Canterbury would have been used for music and magazines.

A Regency sofa, c. 1810. The terms sofa, couch, day bed, chaise longue, settle and settee all describe long seat furniture.

globes. In a country estate office, the special pieces commissioned to act as filing cabinets and partitioned desks and tables for keeping well-ordered records of the surrounding land and its tenants, provide us with a supply of 'one-off' pieces. Double chairs, settees, night tables, chests of drawers, bureaux with secretaire rather than slope-front compartments, hanging shelves and wall and corner cupboards and, by 1800, a loo table for gaming, went to make up the rest of the contents in the well-furnished home together with paintings, mirrors, clocks, a barometer and working models of scientific or educational interest.

Regency mahogany and rosewood crossbanded sofa table with high stretcher and reeded downswept legs with brass cappings. Contemporary cheval mirrors (tall swivel dressing mirrors) had supports and legs of the same kind, and during the late nineteenth and early twentieth centuries were often 'married' to later Regency sofa table tops.

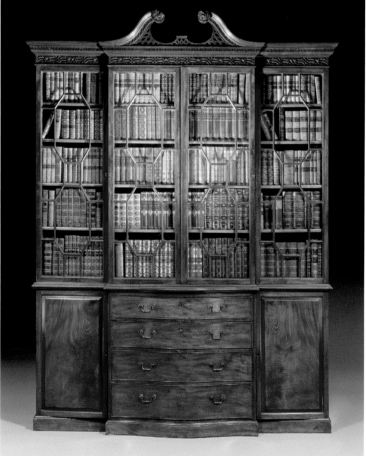

Above left:
A George III mahogany reading or 'Gainsborough type' open armchair, 1775.

Above right:
A Regency mahogany and satinwood banded sofa table on lyre end supports, with low stretcher, lion's paw brass cappings and castors.

Left:
A George III mahogany serpentine break-front bookcase. By this time such cabinets were made in three parts, the end wings being generally set back to give the break-front effect. The upper part with pierced broken swan pediment was added in the late nineteenth century.

Above: An early George III mahogany card table with fold-over top. The rectangular top has rounded projecting corners, and the cabriole legs have bell flower and acanthus carving above claw and ball feet, c. 1765.

Above: A giltwood and marquetry card table from c. 1770, attributed to Pierre Langlois. (Syon House / The Bridgeman Art Library)

Left: A George III Regency mahogany library table with drum top from 1810. The four splayed feet have pronounced leaf carved knees, brass lion's paw cappings and castors.

Chapter Four

THE DESIGNERS

FASHIONABLE ARCHITECTS, designers and cabinet-makers had a tremendous following during the eighteenth century, many attaining huge wealth and positions of high social standing. The economy went from strength to strength under the Whig administration and the signing of the Treaty of Paris in 1763 signalled the end of the Seven Years War with France, opening up new areas for commercial expansion and heralding a greater French influence in design. It was fashionable for educated people to show interest in history and appreciation of the arts; groups of like-minded acquaintances would follow similar lines of study. By the end of the eighteenth century, society was as complex as it is today. On the one hand were the 'avant-garde' extremists and on the other the staid aristocracy unconcerned with all but established good taste: between were the wealthy but obscure, trying to sustain the standards of both. The less affluent middle classes had their own standards and aspirations, while the labouring classes and the poor as always were poor and unaffected by change. This was an era when English design and manufacture reached a peak of diversity, innovation and excellence.

The desire for homes built and furnished *à la mode* grew as increasing numbers of affluent people undertook the 'Grand Tour'. They returned home with eyes educated to appreciate fine art, some knowledge of the latest medical and scientific advances and their heads filled with the current whimsical asymmetrical designs and ponderous proportions of baroque style. These European styles gained a limited but important popularity in England, particularly among the highly influential clients of Daniel Marot and William Kent.

Trade publications not only on building and architecture but also on furniture designs had begun to appear in the late seventeenth century. Leading manufacturers and designers produced and sold books of their designs which were copied by craftsmen throughout the land as far as their skill, materials, and the money at their disposal would allow.

DANIEL MAROT

One of the first to publish his designs for both buildings and the furniture to fill them was Daniel Marot *c.* 1660–1752, a Huguenot who left his native France to seek asylum in Holland. He was already well known as an architect and furniture designer and before long was working for William, Prince of Orange. In 1684, Marot came to England and continued working under the patronage of James II. He is probably best known for his designs of corner chimney pieces with graduated shelves above, and elaborate and intricately carved chair frames, but these were just two among many of his adaptations from the heavy and ornate Louis XIV style. A book of Marot's designs published in the early eighteenth century shows considerable use of sumptuous drapery for curtains, bed hangings, chairs and stools. His designs for the 'show wood' parts of

Opposite:
A room with an ornate plasterwork ceiling at Dumfries House. The house was built between 1754 and 1759 by John and Robert Adam. Here the gently flowing curvilinear lines of the chairs and settees show the restrained elements of the rococo movement, in contrast to the extravagant forms of the girandole to the right of the fireplace and the picture frame on the right, which are more usually associated with it. (Country Life Picture Library)

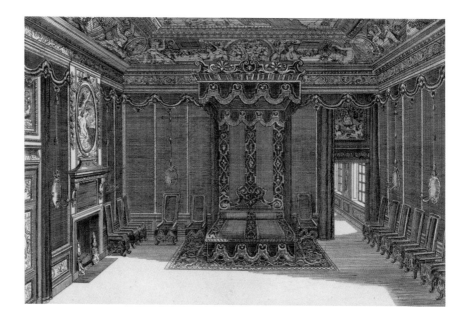

furniture show frequent use of *amorini* (cherubs), masks, torsos and figures, at the same time incorporating many of the patterns already mentioned such as the bow or hoop stretcher rail, the inverted cup and straight taper turning and the curved front leg.

WILLIAM KENT

William Kent (1685–1748) was probably the first true English interior designer. He revolutionised the plans of houses and designed furniture specifically for them. Kent just wished to be an artist and had been sent to Italy to study painting, but this was not where his greatest talent lay. He returned to England in 1719, having met his lifelong friend and patron Richard, third Earl of Burlington, who recognised and encouraged Kent's true gift for architecture. Kent's houses were designed on Palladian lines: each had a grand entrance hall, approached from outer steps, and a succession of rooms leading one into another. Among the great Palladian houses still to be enjoyed today, with their accent on classical lines, porticoes and the five orders are Houghton Hall and Holkham Hall in Norfolk. Interior door pillars and cornices or 'over-doors', although made of wood, had the lines and proportions of masonry, as did much of Kent's furniture. Here the shading and colours of the timber, made more pronounced with the passing of time, can be seen to enhance and heighten the effects of the curved details of the pillared and pedimented bookcases and cabinets. Kent also made considerable use of ponderous and ornate new baroque designs for many large console tables, mirror frames and chairs in the homes he built and furnished, as well as determining all plaster detailing, picture frames, door and chimney furniture, carpets, curtains and wall coverings.

MATTHIAS LOCK AND HENRY COPLAND

Maker, carver, gilder and designer Matthias Lock, who trained as a silver engraver, and his aide, Henry Copland, were two eminent English pioneers of the rococo style. Each renowned in his own right, they collaborated in 1752 to produce a highly influential book, *A New Book of Ornaments*. They were the first Englishmen to publish designs in the newly developed rococo style and from 1740 the design books they produced showed asymmetrical and symmetrical carving of all manner of motifs, the 'C' scroll playing a most important part.

WILLIAM HALLETT

Among the earliest to publish his work was practising cabinet-maker William Hallett, whose rococo furniture was considered the height of fashion in the second quarter of the eighteenth century. He was employed by Lord Folkestone, the Earl of Leicester and the Earl of Pembroke and, it is believed, also by the Duke of Chandos during the building of Canons, near Edgware in Middlesex, described by Defoe as 'the most magnificent palace in England'. By 1745, the Duke's vast fortune had dissipated and his successor demolished the house and sold the materials and fittings. William Hallett bought the estate and much of the materials and built himself an elegant house on the site of the old one. Hallett's son William predeceased him and his grandson, also William, inherited Canons and the estate. By 1786, the grandson had reached such a social position that Thomas Gainsborough painted his portrait with his wife, entitled *The Morning Walk*. Canons is of greatest interest in this context because the doors and panelling were of mahogany; this was one of the earliest recorded uses in large quantity of this newly imported timber.

THOMAS CHIPPENDALE

Undoubtedly the most quoted of mid-eighteenth-century designers is Thomas Chippendale. Born in Yorkshire in 1718, the son of a joiner on a country estate, it can be assumed that Chippendale was sent to London as an apprentice cabinet-maker, for little is known of him before 1748 when he married Catherine Redshaw at St George's Chapel, Hyde Park, London. He rented large London premises, including workshops, a timber store and a front shop, in St Martin's Lane, where he entered into a partnership first with James Rannie, and secondly with Thomas Haig. Chippendale was the first to publish a book composed entirely of furniture designs. *The Gentleman and Cabinet-Maker's Director*, published in 1754, included 160 fine line engravings showing every conceivable type of furniture, decorated or formed after the rococo, Gothic and Chinese tastes. While it contained many fantastic creations that were probably never produced, more importantly there were designs for both ordinary and the most elaborate furniture, which showed popular decorative motifs as being suitable for both. The open-fret cut brackets, the 'cluster column' leg, the gadroon carved edge or the arch shaped open back of a chair are some typical examples that appear on both plain and fancy pieces. The *Director* was not only the first publication to be entirely devoted to furniture, it was the first

A 'Toylet' table, from Thomas Chippendale's Gentleman's Cabinet Directory, 1755. *(See also text on page 99.) (The Stapleton Collection / The Bridgeman Art Library)*

A satinwood and marquetry decorated commode by Thomas Chippendale, the two panels of ebony and ivory depicting 'Diana and Minerva', 1773. (Harewood House / The Bridgeman Art Library)

to include designs that could be achieved by the country craftsman as well as the more sophisticated city cabinet-maker. Justifiably, it became a best-seller. Indeed, it was so popular that it was reprinted in 1755, a weekly series was published from 1759, and it was reproduced as a single, third enlarged edition in 1762. However, some of the greatest pieces to come from Chippendale's workshop were never published in the *Director*, for they were made to the designs of Robert Adam.

By the early 1760s, a classical revival had begun to replace rococo, and it was in this style that Chippendale produced some of his greatest work. First through carving and later by reviving the use of marquetry, he interpreted classical motifs in a display of controlled craftsmanship unsurpassed before or since.

ROBERT ADAM

The accession in 1760 of George III, grandson of George II, had little effect on the sweeping changes of fashion from rococo to Classical. Indeed, such was the King's preference for the simpler things in life that he was nick-named 'Farmer George'. At the time of the accession, the young architect Robert Adam was completing his artistic and architectural education in Italy, drawing inspiration from the baths of Caracalla and Diocletian, Hadrian's villa at Tivoli, and the basilicas and vaulted temples at Herculaneum, which he visited in 1754. His interpretations would affect the work of English craftsmen during the next decade.

Whereas Kent's designs had adhered more strictly to the original, Adam's designs were a definite, personalised version of the Classical. It is interesting to compare

One of two Robert Adam designs for a painted Breakfasting Room, 1768, for Kedleston Hall, Derbyshire. (National Trust Photographic Library/John Hammond/ The Bridgeman Art Library)

these to the neo-classical movement of 1799–1830 in which the designs hardly deviated from the Roman and Italian models. But the basic ideas were the same – simplicity and elegance in outline, the appearance of height and space and the use of geometrically balanced curved arches and tapering columns. For detailing, Adam used such motifs as husks, urns, festoons, the anthemion (or honeysuckle), and ram's-head masks in the door furniture, wall hangings, mantelpieces, overdoors and cornices, as well as in the carpets, furniture, silver, fine cut glass and porcelain. The contemporary work of Matthew Boulton, Hester Bateman the silversmith, and the potter Josiah Wedgwood are typical examples of Adam's amazing influence across the entire field of the decorative arts.

WILLIAM INCE AND JOHN MAYHEW

As cabinet-makers and upholsterers, this partnership dominated the second half of the eighteenth century in highest quality production. It is also one of the best documented companies, for litigation in the early nineteenth century necessitated the recording of entries and accounts over the years of their business together, giving us, ironically, a detailed insight into the lives and practices of a large and prestigious furnishing company during the Georgian era.

Between 1759 and 1763, Ince and Mayhew published the *Universal System of Household Furniture*. This contained 300 designs and owed much to Chippendale's *Director*, but shows inspired elegance and some very sound advice to any 'gentleman who may furnish as neat at a small expense as he can elegant and superb at a great one'. A major client was the ninth Earl of Exeter, and some magnificent examples of Ince and Mayhew's work can be seen in the state rooms in Burghley House at Stamford in Lincolnshire, particularly the Gothic pews in the chapel.

GEORGE HEPPLEWHITE

Much early classical period furniture shows the use of incised and applied carving on plain mahogany, but by 1770 veneer work had again become popular and so had its natural partner, marquetry. Some of the finest marquetry of this period was executed to designs of Robert Adam by Thomas Chippendale. Furniture made strictly to Adam's designs was intended only for the great country and London houses where he and his contemporary followers were employed at the time. And, just as the rococo, Gothic and chinoiserie styles had been presented to furniture makers throughout the country by Thomas Chippendale, so the designs of Adam spread to a far wider field through the work of George Hepplewhite. Comparatively little is known of this man, and it is largely because of the 300 illustrations published in his *Cabinet-Maker and Upholsterer's Guide* in 1788, two years after his death, that his name is so famous.

A George III carved mahogany open armchair from 1790 with shield back, in the manner of Hepplewhite.

That Hepplewhite had practical knowledge of a workshop is substantiated by the fact that he was at one time an apprentice to the firm of Gillows of Lancaster, and by 1760 had established a shop in Cripplegate in London. The *Guide* was actually published by Hepplewhite's widow, Alice, and was such a success that a second edition was published in 1789 and a third in 1794. Hepplewhite only incorporated those designs of Adam he thought most suitable for furniture. There appear no military trophies or ram's-head masks on Hepplewhite's designs. The use of classical scenes painted in panels to form the focal point of the article was excluded, too. He made use of oval and round paterae (carved and, usually, applied discs), swags, husks, flower and bell festoons, and fluting and, although he did not invent them, he certainly popularised the stylised heart and the shield as shapes for chair backs. He almost certainly introduced the use of simulated Prince of Wales feathers as a motif, used concurrently, but not on the same piece, as ears of wheat, although the idea might have stemmed from the designs for some chair backs by James Wyatt, a young and successful architect of the period. At the same time there was a strong French influence, which can be seen in the curving lines of the small window seats and open armchairs of this style between 1770 and 1790. As this was, like most influences, a modified version attributed to a leading designer of the time in the country, it is generally referred to as 'French' Hepplewhite.

THOMAS SHERATON

The best examples of the straight, tapering legs, delicacy of framework and generally fine proportions of furniture which epitomised the late eighteenth century, were the work of Thomas Sheraton. His *Cabinet-Maker and Upholsterer's Drawing Book,* which was published in three parts from 1791 to 1794, presents us with the most comprehensive picture available of good-quality, late-eighteenth-century furniture.

Born in Stockton-on-Tees in 1751, it is believed that Sheraton came to London during the early 1790s. He was trained as a practising cabinet-maker, but there is to date no proof that he actually made furniture to his own designs. However, his work was so greatly respected that his ideas were reproduced by contemporary quality craftsmen all over England, which is why the majority of quality furniture of this time is referred to as 'Sheraton'. An extremely competent draughtsman, he was the author of various works on philosophy and religion, too. Sheraton's great talent was his ability to take points of style and decoration from his predecessors as well as his contemporaries, and

A George III rosewood crossbanded and sycamore marquetry demi-lune commode. The doors are centred with classical urns.

A late George III mahogany window seat in the manner of Hepplewhite, with over scrolled ends above an upholstered seat. The tapering stop fluted legs have brass cappings and castors.

then to blend them in such a way as to produce styles of unique elegance in English furniture. After the turn of the century, he became more affected by the formal classical movement, and in 1802 published the *Cabinet Dictionary*. Within its pages he illustrated the French and Grecian styles, and advocated much use of animal figures, torsos, heads and feet as important features. This was an innovation which affected both fine and more ordinary furniture. For example, a plain brass castor was cast realistically to represent a lion's paw – a pattern that remained popular until the 1820s. At about this time the acanthus leaf became a popular alternative.

A Sheraton harewood and marquetry serpentine commode, c. 1790 (Partridge Fine Arts / The Bridgeman Art Library)

HENRY HOLLAND

At the end of the eighteenth century there was, among *cognoscenti*, a preference towards pure classical designs in contrast to the modified versions of Adam. It was at this time that what is known today as the neo-classical movement began. This was especially encouraged by the interest in the arts shown by George, Prince of Wales who, at the age of 21, employed the architect and designer Henry Holland to furnish Carlton House, the Prince's London residence. Holland had married Bridget, daughter of the great landscape gardener, Capability Brown, and was thus introduced to top-level clients, particularly Whig members of the famous Brook's Club in St James's, where the Prince was a member. Holland's designs were deemed outlandish by the followers of the more genteel Adam and Sheraton patterns, which in itself appealed to the avante-garde Prince. Based on contemporary French, antique Graeco-Roman and Chinese originals, Holland used strongly figured veneer-gilded bronze and wood, as well as dark painted panels and lacquer to give even more impact to his furniture. Henry Holland remained architect and principal furniture designer to the Prince from 1783 until his death in 1806, and so distinctive was his style that we now refer to furniture made to his designs from this period through until 1830 as 'Regency' although the political regency of his patron was only from 1811–20.

THOMAS HOPE

Thomas Hope was more than merely a designer, more than a promoter of the decorative arts and more than simply a patron whose wealth sponsored the talents of others: Hope was a combination of all three. While his name is often connected with a minor and somewhat eccentric furtherance of the Egyptian taste, Hope produced some most influential designs for furniture and interior decoration in the

purest (it was claimed) Egyptian, Grecian and Roman styles. Essentially these were for use in his homes in Duchess Street, London, and later The Deepdene near Dorking in Surrey. Both houses were altered to display his collections of classical bronzes, vases and other antiquities, and the furniture and settings were intended to enhance them. In order to encourage this taste, Hope published a book of his own drawings, *Household Furniture and Interior Decoration*, in 1807. This showed his outstanding ability as a draughtsman and designer, from complete room schemes to separate pieces of furniture and individual motifs. Hope incorporated and popularised many embellishments of the French Empire period, and the use of black and coloured paint with gilding in the manner of the ancient Egyptians.

GEORGE SMITH

At the beginning of the nineteenth century, more people than ever were able to afford fashionable and material comforts, and the selection available was much wider and more varied than before. Cabinet-maker and upholsterer George Smith was one of the chief exponents of the modified versions of the high Regency style which appealed to the new, larger clientele, and his first major work, *A Collection of Designs for Household Furniture and Interior Decoration*, published in 1808, has become an essential reference for the connoisseur of the market in this period. His excessive use of animal figures, such as the sphinx, griffins, leopards and lions together with acanthus and palm leaf motifs can be said to typify the main essence of Regency, and he was careful to record the revival of lacquer, both Chinese and Japanese, of caning for chair-backs and seats and of buhl, the inlay of brass and tortoiseshell. His last book, *The Cabinet-Maker and Upholsterer's Guide* (1826–27) shows designs that were to be the basis for much Victorian furniture during the ensuing sixty years.

Below:
A mahogany cylinder-fall writing desk with bookcase, c. 1805. The quadrant section cover folded back into the desk and a writing platform could be pulled forward by means of the second row of knobs.

GEORGE SEDDON

Of the successful cabinet-makers who achieved great wealth and eminence in society, a notable example is George Seddon (1727–1801), who, by 1786, employed some 400 craftsmen. These included locksmiths, gilders, upholsterers, carvers and mirror makers, and in December 1789, Seddon's annual stock-take totalled £118,926, a phenomenal amount. At the time of his death, he was acknowledged as having the largest-scale cabinet-making business ever known, a record which has scarcely been broken since.

GILLOWS OF LANCASTER

Any piece of furniture bearing a contemporary label that gives clues as to its origin is obviously considerably more interesting from a historical point of view. Sadly, though, the practice of signing, stamping and labelling furniture was less popular in England than it was in France until the nineteenth century when, during the 1820s, more and more of the leading manufacturers and retailers took up this display of pride in, or responsibility for, their merchandise. Comparatively few eighteenth-century cabinet-makers signed, labelled or stamped their work, and so pieces made by those who did will have an enhanced historical and commercial value. But only up to a point, for the majority of such makers have failed to become household names. In commercial terms it works this way. Take, for instance, an early George III bureau with no attribution to a maker, no documentary evidence of provenance or verifiable family history. Call this category 1. Depending on its quality and condition it will have a set market price for its type. Say it is good quality with original feet and handles, of mahogany with fine patination and colour; its price would be between £5,000 and £7,000 (an arbitrary figure).

A pair of Regency mahogany open armchairs with reed turned and tapering legs in the manner of Gillows, 1810.

Now imagine the same bureau but with a maker's label fixed somewhere inside. The increase in price – not to be confused with historical value – will be governed by the present-day cognisance and popularity of that maker. If it is a maker from the provinces about whom little is known, or perhaps a city craftsman better known in his day than he is now, such a label will increase the price by 15 to 20 per cent only. If, on the other hand, the label is of a cabinet-maker who was renowned in his own time, whose work career is documented and whose famous clients are listed, then that label (or stamp) – which in itself may need to be authenticated – can at least double the category 1 price.

One prime example of this is the family firm of Gillows of Lancaster

and London (*c.* 1730 to post-1840). Later to become better known as Waring & Gillow, the famous London store, the company began stamping its wares 'Gillows – Lancaster' about 1780. They continued to produce all manner of goods, all of the highest quality in both timber and construction, to established patterns and to new designs throughout the nineteenth century. Among those was the recorded manufacture in the late eighteenth century of the Davenport desk for a Captain Davenport. More important at the time was their patented 'Imperial Extending Dining Table' in 1800, which gained them a huge clientele. Various illustrations from their later pattern books and catalogues illustrate their immense range and show that they also produced out-of-period pieces in the mid eighteenth-century style. These are well worth looking out for.

Above left:
A late George IV or early William IV mahogany bedroom table and washstand by Gillow & Co. on turned and tapering legs, 1825–40. The holes are for various bowls and other receptacles.

Above right:
A William IV figured oak Davenport by Gillows on lobed bun feet with castors, 1835.

GEORGE BULLOCK

It seems that each period also produces at least one designer or maker whose attribution sends the price of a piece of furniture soaring, even when that attribution is based on stylistic or constructional similarities or documentation rather than the hard evidence of a label or stamp. The effect is enlarged by a comparatively small output for an élite clientele. While Thomas Chippendale's designs were copied nationwide, any authentic pieces known to have been made by him or in his workshops are almost beyond price. In the same way, but to a lesser degree thus far, in the Regency era the name of George Bullock stands out above all others. Known to have lived in Liverpool and London between *c.* 1777 and his premature death in 1818, Bullock produced what can only be described as dramatic furniture in the classic high-style Regency tradition, after Henry Holland but incorporating buhl work, fine metal mounts and native timbers. His revival of the use of oak, in veneers as well as in the solid, was to have an influence on the furniture trade for the rest of the nineteenth century. His designs were published frequently in Ackermann's *Repository* during his lifetime, particularly while he was based in London. In addition, his output as a painter, sculptor, designer and creator of works of art in marble was prolific, and he was greatly mourned when he died.

Chapter Five

DECORATION

BY THE TIME George IV died in 1830, the taste for Old French, particularly that of the Louis XIV period, was deeply entrenched in society circles. The interior of Crockford's Club underwent a total interior design and redecoration in that style in 1827. The décor was the work of Philip and Benjamin Dean Wyatt, and within three years the French taste had become popular for most fashionable boudoirs and feminine apartments, whilst the heavier and more formal 'Modern Greek' was still considered proper for the masculine rooms. It is with these two overriding styles that the complex pattern of the Victorian age began. This would soon change, however, with the introduction of more and more ancient English and other foreign influences in a period of industrial invention and the greatest exhibitions the world had ever seen, beginning with the Great Exhibition of 1851.

The use of classical motifs on the heavier furniture of the late Regency gave way to carved, stylised floral motifs on much the same basic shapes. The lotus leaf, which was a popular motif of the period, is a particularly notable example. For a comprehensive view of designs for furniture and interior decoration of the period, Rudolph Ackermann's *Repository of the Arts*, generally known as Ackermann's *Repository*, and George Smith's final publication, *The Cabinet-Maker and Upholsterer's Guide* of 1828, are among the best sources.

DECORATION AND MATERIALS

Towards the end of the eighteenth century, English furniture made of mahogany, and in the French taste, for the most part was left undecorated, while if it was made in pine or beech it was either gilded or painted with white or pastel colours, which could be enhanced with gilt. At the same time, and thereafter, an enormous variety of highly decorative timbers were used, both in the solid and for veneers. These can be classified as belonging to one of three main recognisable types: those of essentially uniform colour but with great depth, like certain cuts of mahogany, satinwood, oak, maple, harewood and ebony; those with contrasting streaks in the grain such as rosewood, kingwood, zebrawood, tulipwood and coromandel; and those with the burr of pollarded figuring such as amboyna, elder, elm, maple, yew and oak.

Exotic veneers were further accentuated with painted panels depicting mythological and classical scenes by such artists as Antonio Zucchi, Angelica Kauffman and Michele Angelo Pergolesi, or they were created in fine marquetry, which saw a renaissance. Satinwood and rosewood are, of course, the woods most usually associated with the last quarter of the eighteenth century, but there were many other beautiful woods available to the craftsmen of the time. The species of satinwood (*Xanthoxylum flavum*) used on the finest quality furniture came from the West Indies. It had a fine golden yellow colour, a hard undulating grain and such depth that it closely resembled satin material when cut and polished. Such wood was used for veneering on to mahogany, oak or

Opposite:
A George IV buhl and ebonised gilt bronze mounted occasional table in the manner of the Blake Family, London, 1825. The pattern of scrolls and foliage is typical of buhl work. (See also page 84 illustration)

A George IV rosewood and parcel gilt console table from 1825 with classical lion's head and supports on paw feet, typical of the late Regency period. The grey marble top is above a central mirrored back and sides.

A Victorian French-inspired carved rosewood and upholstered sofa, 1860.

pine until the latter part of the century when Sheraton suggested its use in the solid. A second type of satinwood (*Chloroxylon swietenia*) was imported from the East Indies, but this did not come into general use for furniture until the early part of the nineteenth century. It had a more shallow lemon colour with closer, smaller markings, and lacked the richness of the West Indian variety.

Rosewood came firstly from the West Indies and later the East Indies and Brazil. Like satinwood, it was used for veneer and decoration before being used in the solid. It is generally a dark wood with red-brown streaks accentuated by darker brown or black markings.

Detail of cresting on a George III chair, showing gesso under gilding. See also page 29.

This photo of the drawing room at Arundel Castle shows an ormolu pier table and looking glass in the high style rococo manner. (His Grace The Duke of Norfolk, Arundel Castle/The Bridgeman Art Library)

The covering of protective polish that was applied to most furniture at this time has allowed some rosewood articles to attain a mellow and well-figured appearance. If this original polish is removed, however, rosewood tends to turn black and much of its beauty can be lost. Kingwood (*Dalbergia cearensis*), tulipwood (*Dalbergia variabilis*) and zebrawood (*Connarus guianensis*) were all used as veneers for panels and banding rather than in the solid. Kingwood is more like satinwood in general colour and appearance, for its tendency to fade has lessened the contrast between the dark and light markings which, when the wood is freshly cut, vary from deep brown to pale yellow. Tulipwood, also known as 'white poplar', is the light soft wood of the tulip tree, and zebrawood is a hard, close-grained timber with fairly close and very pronounced markings of yellow and dark brown. Numerous books on woods are now available in libraries and bookshops.

ORMOLU

By the time the word 'ormolu' was used in England in the latter part of the eighteenth century, it was discontinued in France in favour of the term *bronze d'ore*. This accounts for the supposition in England that ormolu applies only to work executed in gilt bronze. This is not necessarily true; ormolu can be any fine gilt metal, for the derivation is from *or moulu* – ground gold – therefore either gilt brass or bronze can be described as ormolu. The main method of applying the gold was mercurial gilding. This is done by mixing gold and mercury to form an amalgam, applying it to the surface of the metal which is then heated to evaporate the mercury and leave the gold firmly fixed. (This method is no longer used as the fumes from evaporating mercury can be lethal.)

METAL MOUNTS

Iron locks had been used on chests in England since the fourteenth century. These comprised an encased interior mechanism and a front panel which, during the fifteenth century, it became fashionable to decorate. By the sixteenth century there had been such advances in lock-making that cupboards for downstairs rooms were fitted with concealed locks with keyhole protection and disguise created by a plate escutcheon. Either as part of this plate or fixed separately, a wrought, inverted heart-shaped handle was attached, and this remained quite usual on country furniture until the early part of the eighteenth century. During the latter part of the seventeenth century, however, the forging of mounts for fine furniture and locksmithing became independent occupations distinct from that of the general blacksmith. The Oriental lacquered furniture that was imported in such vast quantities after the Restoration bore large, double-plate escutcheons, corner guards and angle straps of thin gilded brass, decorated with flat-chased foliate designs. Naturally, as increasing amounts of imitation lacquered furniture were produced in England, so the metal mounts had also to be reproduced. For a time, the quality and appearance of the original eluded the English manufacturers, but the importance of metalwork on furniture had been established and the need to use materials other than iron, particularly for drawer handles and escutcheon plates.

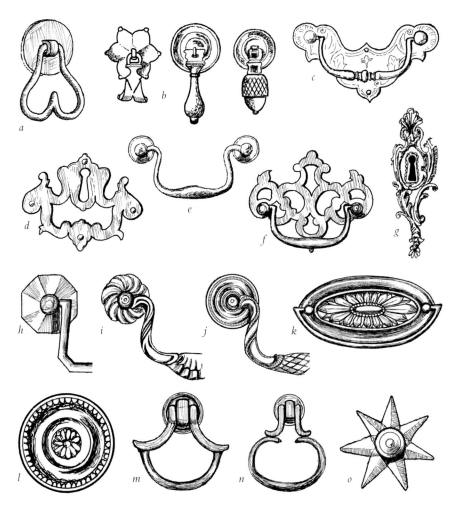

Some typical handles of the seventeenth, eighteenth and nineteenth centuries. (a) Iron inverted heart-shape drop handle, early seventeenth century. (b) Brass pendant handles, early eighteenth century. (c) Engraved back-plate loop handle of cast brass, early eighteenth century. (d) Pierced escutcheon, later part of first half of eighteenth century. (e) Loop or swan-neck handle of cast brass, second half of eighteenth century. (f) Pierced back-plate loop handle, c. 1760. (g) Cast brass escutcheon in the rococo manner, mid-eighteenth century. (h) Cast brass loop handle with octagonal rose, French style, second half of the eighteenth century. (i) and (j) Two types of decoratively cast and chased loop handles with roses, later eighteenth century. (k) Stamped sheet brass back-plate loop handle, after c. 1780. (l) Stamped brass knob with screw fixing, late eighteenth century. (m) Cast brass drop handle, c. 1775–1800. (n) Cast brass drop handle, c. 1750–75. (o) Regency period star knob.

Until the latter part of the eighteenth century, metal mounts of this type were cast from a mould, 'finished' by a chaser and engraver and then either polished and lacquered or gilded. Although gilt metal mounts of finest quality were produced in France from the end of the seventeenth century, it is not until the 1760s and after that the equivalent or anything like it was produced in England.

The development of the metal mount industry in England and, at one time, the sale of English ormolu to France, can mainly be attributed to one man, Matthew Boulton (1728–1802). From his workshops in Soho, Birmingham, Boulton produced innovative silver plate wares and the finest ormolu, which made him one of the leading figures in the development of sophisticated metalware production in England. His mounts for furniture were held to be among the very best and so were used by all the leading designers and makers. At this time, the mounting of semi-precious stone, particularly 'Blue John', to form *cassolets* (decorative candlesticks of classical shape on which the sconces can be reversed to form pot-pourri vases) became popular. Blue John takes its name from a corruption of the French description of its colour, *bleu-jaune*, and is a fibrous variety of Derbyshire fluorspar stone found only in that part of the world.

The other significant development was in the castors or small wheels which enabled furniture to be moved easily from one place to another. A simple form of castor was no doubt in use for some special pieces of furniture as early as the sixteenth century, but the potential benefit of such a fitting was not recognised until the end of the seventeenth century. At this time, a wooden wheel on an axle between two plates, secured to a swivelling pin which allowed movement in any direction, was introduced, and by the early eighteenth century small, hardwood rollers were in general use on good domestic furniture. During the 1740s and 1750s, the rollers were made of leather rather than wood, and consisted of several washers placed together on the axle, the swivelling pin being secured to a brass plate which was screwed to the underside of the foot. While ball-and-claw and

A George IV buhl and ebonised gilt bronze mounted occasional table in the manner of the Blake Family, London, 1825. The pattern of scrolls and foliage is typical of buhl work. See also page 78.

pad feet provided space enough for this plate, the tapering legs and feet of the post-1760 period did not, and a cup-type castor that fitted over the end of the leg was introduced. After around 1770, this was all made of brass, including the wheel, and the 'cup' was of square form. Later this was made to taper in line with the leg. Castors of the 1775–1800 period often copied the spade-shape feet which were so popular at this time. The cup castor on the horizontal, as in the case of a tripod base, was also introduced at the same time. The first of this kind was basically rectangular with the upper two edges slightly chamfered, and its shape following the end of the line of the leg. An alternative was the same shape but with a raised lip. Soon after the turn of the century a realistically cast lion's paw became the most popular, but by 1820 this had been replaced by the formal acanthus leaf and other stylised foliate motifs of the period. All these patterns were revived towards the end of the nineteenth century.

During the Regency period, burr veneers of oak, yew and maple were extremely popular, and after 1815 panels of buhl work appeared, reintroduced by French craftsmen, particularly Louis Gaigneur who opened premises in London and supplied to the Prince Regent a writing table decorated with buhl. From then on it remained fashionable in varying degrees, terminating in a deluge of mass production in the 1870s.

A George IV mahogany dining chair with inverted lotus leaf cap on front legs, from 1828.

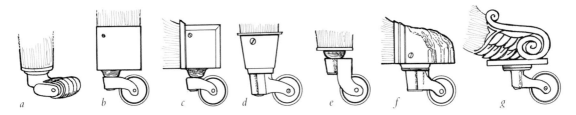

(a) Castor with wheel made of leather discs, c. 1740–60. Used for ball and claw feet and square untapered legs. (b) Square cup castor, c. 1760–75, by which time it was generally made of brass. (c) The plain toe castor on the horizontal used for the spreading legs of the tripod and four splay table bases. From 1790 if tapered. (d) The tapered cup castor with a top protruding lip often replaced the spade foot for turned and square legs, from 1785. (e) A small brass castor, used on small pieces of furniture during the last quarter of the eighteenth century. (f) The lion's paw castor, 1800–20, but a most popular replacement for later, or reproduction furniture. (g) A typical late-Regency stylised foliate cup castor, c. 1820–35.

CONTINUING INFLUENCES OF PAST STYLE

During the short reign of William IV and the early years of Victoria's reign (from 1837), there was a great expansion in the furniture industry. The pattern of development, apparent from the sixteenth century, in which the introduction, improvement and inevitable over-elaboration of a style was followed by a modified revival of an earlier fashion, can be seen to continue throughout the Victorian and early Edwardian periods. However, mechanisation enabled the production of furniture in a greater variety of styles and quality than ever before and so makes it far more difficult to chronicle both the structure and patterns of furniture fashions.

The more architectural elements of the classical antique popularised during the Regency period (1784–1830, the period influenced by the young Prince George rather than just the nine years of constitutional Regency, 1811–20) by such men as Henry Holland, Thomas Hope, George Smith, George Bullock and Richard Brown continued to dominate the more masculine apartments in fashionable houses well into the 1840s. Examples can be found dating from later in the nineteenth century but they cannot be regarded as typical of contemporary fashions. These designs are referred to as Grecian or Egyptian, the latter being the more truly descriptive, and can be recognised by such motifs as the unbroken pediment, curved corner bracket (*acroter*), formalised lotus and acanthus leaf capping to columns and side supports, and the continued popularity of the sarcophagus shape. One visible change that occurred during the 1820–40 period was that the 'bas-relief' carving of the decorative motif became heavier and later even cumbersome. The timber most popular for furniture made in this style was Honduras, San Domingo and Mexican mahogany, French polished to a glossy finish and reddish colour.

At this time there were three other major sources of inspiration for furniture designers and architects: medieval, Elizabethan and Old French. The medieval taste is also referred to as Gothic, for it is this mock ecclesiastical aspect which formed the basis of many of the purer medieval furniture designs. In a Gothic revival during the Regency period, cluster columns, exaggerated arches and crenellations provided the main theme, to which might be added portcullises, simulated masonry and iron or steel strapwork. The styles of Perpendicular, Curvilinear, Geometric and Decorated periods of church architecture are all represented, with quatrefoil and lancet window shapes and crocket decoration to spires and towers being among the most popular. These patterns were employed for both the basic shape and the decoration of all types of furniture as well as architecture during the 1840s and 1850s. The finest example by one of the leading exponents of this taste, Augustus Welby Northmore Pugin (1812–52), is the close detail and interior decoration of the Houses of Parliament (ceremonially opened in 1852).

Pugin's gothic furniture from Ackermann's Repository of Arts, Literature, Commerce, Manufactures, Fashion and Politics, *published from 1809 to 1828. The height of the Gothic Revival is clear in this image. (The Bridgeman Art Library)*

A set of six Victorian rosewood parlour or dining chairs with balloon backs and upholstered seats, 1860. Examples of this type can be found dating from the mid-1830s well into the 1860s.

'Elizabethan' design was purely Victorian in concept, for it shows the fascination the Victorians had for the original English Renaissance and the earlier Romanesque periods, and their apparent love of the overdecorated pastiche. Rooms were panelled in oak and furnished with heavily carved buffets, cupboards, sideboards, tables and chairs in such profusion as could never have been envisaged previously. Much of the carving depicts Victorianised Elizabethan figures in romantic settings, surmounted by sentries, guardian angels often in apparent distress, supported by bacchanalian torsos amid Italian- and French-style curves and scrolls.

By the late 1820s, designs in the 'Old French' taste were based mainly on the Louis XIV period, but during the 1830s practically all the important French designs of the eighteenth and early nineteenth century were employed, hence its nickname, *Tous-les-Louis*, or 'all the Louis'. Philip and Benjamin Dean Wyatt's redecoration of Crockford's Club in 1827 showed total devotion to the French taste in furnishing as well as décor, as evidenced by the deeply curving frames for chairs and settees, luxurious drapes of richly braided and figured velours and elaborate stucco work to walls and ceilings displaying cherubs and mythical characters in abundance. This was indeed the origin of the curved-leg and oval-backed parlour and dining chairs which today seem to typify 'Victoriana', and which in the past have often been mis-described as 'Queen Anne'. This style of décor remained popular until the end of the century and can still be seen in some of the older, grander hotels in London and Paris.

Chapter Six

WILLIAM IV AND EARLY QUEEN VICTORIA

WILLIAM IV, 1830–7

WILLIAM IV was a kindly man, given to long speeches, and known to his subjects as the 'Sailor King' because of his eleven-year career in the Royal Navy. He had no children. He showed little enthusiasm for changing the course of political history and even less inclination to influence the design and decoration of English furniture. However, by the end of his reign, furniture manufacture in England had grown into a vast industry employing thousands of highly skilled and specialised workers.

QUEEN VICTORIA, 1837–1901

Queen Victoria was the daughter of William's brother Edward, Duke of Kent, fourth son of George III. She was crowned on 28th June 1838 aged 19, and in 1840 married Prince Albert of Saxe-Coburg and Gotha, who was made Prince Consort. They had nine children. During her long reign, which spanned over 63 years until her death in 1901, Britain experienced the most remarkable colonial, commercial, technical and industrial growth in its history. Iron and steel became of vital importance; steam, gas and electricity were harnessed; trains, tramcars and underground railways offered people opportunities for public transport and the first cars were slowly trundling along country lanes. Large hotels were built to accommodate the newly mobile population; letter post, the telegraph and popular newspapers conveyed information faster and more accurately than ever before. The population doubled in just two generations – in the fifteen years prior to the Great Exhibition of 1851, it rose to 18 million. Despite the dire poverty that still afflicted the poorest homes, the Industrial Revolution brought a degree of affluence to a greater section of society than ever before. It was not surprising, therefore, that the furniture industry boomed. By 1850, the earliest type of steam-powered carving machinery was in use, and mass-production was on its way in.

The Victorian age was one of great religious zeal and this often smothering, sometimes pious, enthusiasm did a great deal to keep the demand for ecclesiastical decoration alive. The style is described in the title of one of the many works by A. W. N. Pugin, *The True Principles of Pointed or Christian Architecture* (1841). As a natural reaction to Regency permissiveness, exposure of the female form was kept to a minimum, waists were 'straight-laced' and skirts, once again, became voluminous and, fashioned from rich and heavy materials, were totally unsuited to the delicate furniture of the late eighteenth and early nineteenth centuries. So not

Opposite:
The Morning Room, Castle Ward, County Down, Northern Ireland. Here a library or 'drum' table, with the form of its centre column derived from the Etruscan patterns popular in the 1820s, sits happily with examples of the Gothic Revival evident in the chair backs and cabinet doors. The latter is capped incongruously with a rococo cornice. (National Trust Photographic Library/Andreas von Einsiedel/The Bridgeman Art Library)

89

An ornately carved mahogany and bronze mounted mid-Victorian exhibition-quality sideboard.

only taste but fashion decreed that free-standing or 'occasional' furniture should be built more substantially. During the latter part of the century even the legs of tables, chairs, settees, pianos, chimney pieces and shelves were modestly covered with material, if not upholstered then draped with fitted covers edged with deep fringing.

The re-emergence of Elizabethan style was considerably encouraged by the popularity of romantic novels by Sir Walter Scott, published from 1814 onwards, and a host of factual books about the period. However, this renewed interest was more a matter of entertainment than a thirst for precise knowledge. This is borne out by countless examples of authentic early English furniture, which were cut up and used either in whole or in part to make new pieces that would fit more suitably into the fashionable Victorian house. This practice was so extensive that it was possible to visit premises in all major cities where large stocks of Elizabethan furniture parts, such as chest fronts, bed-posts, drawers and drawer fronts and other decorative sections could be bought already mutilated or dismembered to order. After the commissioned cabinet-maker had done his work, the finished article was often further decorated by a member of the family pursuing the latest pastime of wood carving. This frightening hobby gained rapid popularity after a display at the Great Exhibition in 1851 of work produced by the Warwick School of Carving. English furniture on display at the Crystal Palace illustrated the ultimate fancies of designers and decorators, and the supreme heights of technical achievement in the hands of skilled manufacturers. It also reflected the spirit of England at the time.

THE GREAT EXHIBITION, 1851

The idea of holding public exhibitions in various areas of the decorative arts was not new. As early as 1757, the Society of Arts had offered prizes for the best examples of carpets, porcelain and tapestry and had exhibited the entries. In 1762, the Royal Academy of Painting was established, and since then numerous branches of industry had shown interest in this kind of competitive display. However, until the mid-nineteenth century the French were far more enthusiastic about art exhibitions than the English.

Thanks to the enthusiastic leadership of Henry Cole, the Society of Arts was persuaded to organise three annual exhibitions from 1847 to 1849. Following their success, a deputation from the society met the Lord Mayor of London with plans for holding in 1851 an International Exhibition, and Hyde Park was eventually the site of first choice. This meeting was attended by more than four hundred wealthy bankers and merchants. According to an eye-witness account, the atmosphere was electric and by no means all present were in favour of the proposition. Nevertheless, it was passed and the committee organised a competition for the design of the exhibition hall. The plans were to be submitted within a month. Over 230 enthusiastic architects and designers submitted designs but none was considered suitable, so the Building Committee devised its own plan. This, too, was found to be impracticable but then, only days before the deadline, the firm of Fox and Henderson finalised and submitted detailed drawings of a plan by Joseph Paxton to build an enormous pavilion of glass – the Crystal Palace. Henry Cole persuaded Prince Albert to take an interest, and the Prince became so fascinated by the whole concept that he contributed far more than expected, and thus took most of the credit for the Exhibition's considerable success.

The Crystal Palace was a vast structure of iron and glass, enclosing approximately 19 acres of Hyde Park and tall enough to include its huge elm trees. The galleries and upper bays were to provide one third as much space again to accommodate the 15,000 exhibitors from all over the world. The main entrance led into a huge, vaulted transept with a domed roof and galleries all around. To right and left of this, two wings extended. These were constructed in three, graduated floors, with the flags of all nations flying round the borders. 30 miles of cast-iron frame formed the roof and 900,000 square feet of glass were used to form the shell. To allay any fears of its structural safety, 8-ton wagons of cannonballs were hauled up and down the aisles, and companies of troops marched in closed ranks around the bays. After the Exhibition, the palace was dismantled and re-built in Sydenham and there it remained until 1936 when it burnt to the ground.

The nave of the Great Exhibition, 1851. Among other things, the building showcased many different styles of furniture by varied manufacturers and designers from across Europe. (The Stapleton Collection / The Bridgeman Art Library)

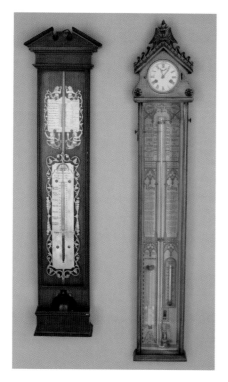

A Victorian Admiral Fitzroy barometer introduced in 1860, which included a sealed storm glass – the contents of which were kept secret by Admiral Fitzroy. This example is from 1870. There are also instructions for making forecasts from natural observations. Fitzroy was the captain of HMS Beagle *during Darwin's famous voyage.*

The displays were split into four categories: Sculpture and Fine Arts, Raw Materials, Machinery and Manufacture. The Exhibition ran from 1 May until 7 October 1851, during which time more than six million visitors came to view more than one million objects on display. It was a huge financial success. Apart from over £60,000 raised by public subscription and £40,000 from the sale of season tickets (£3 for gentlemen, £2 for ladies), Spicer and Clowes paid £32,000 for the right to print catalogues and Schweppes paid over £55,000 for the right to supply refreshments (in the event, more than £75,000 worth of soft drinks and light food was sold). After the first three weeks, the entrance fee was lowered to one shilling on weekdays and 2s 6d, and 5s at weekends.

Even after the Exhibition doors closed, interest in the concept did not die. Every country that had participated brought fresh ideas for interior design and decoration and each had an impact on the English buying public. English furniture history becomes more complicated from this time. New steam-driven machinery revolutionised production in such a way that, for the first time, it was possible for everyone to buy fashionable furniture in a variety of styles directly from a shop, rather than having to commission it from designs in a book.

It was the miles of terraced houses which were being built in all the major towns and cities to house a new, moderately wealthy, middle class that provided the enormous demand for new, shop-bought furniture. Each of these houses had a hall, basement, a front room, a parlour, a kitchen and at least one floor, if not two above. The household was considered incomplete without a resident maid or servant and it was necessary to finish a servant's room with at least a bed, dressing table, pot cupboard and wardrobe. In larger houses, spare bedrooms and conservatories had to be furnished, as did libraries and the new 'smoking rooms' occasioned by the increased popularity of smoking.

THE HALL STAND

One of the most popular items to appear in the early Victorian period was the hall stand. The first of these appeared during the later years of the Regency period as a free-standing turned post with extended arms to take cloaks and hats. It was not until the entrance hall gained prominence in middle-class as well as upper-class houses that this useful article became so much in demand. In the masses of smaller houses, the hall was usually narrow, serving only as access to the downstairs and basement rooms, the staircase and the landing for the upper floors. To make the hall stand more useful without increasing its size, it was placed against the wall, a shelf was built mid-way up the column with a drawer below flanked by racks to take sticks and umbrellas, with iron drip-trays sunk into the base. A mirror was placed in the centre of the back at head height. Made from a variety of materials (cast iron, bamboo and even papier-mâché), the hall-stand could be found in practically every house in the country by the end of the century.

INDOOR PLANTS

The Victorians had a passion for gardens, and conservatories were added to larger houses so that the owners could enjoy all-year-round floral displays or 'winter gardens'. As such extensions were not always possible in smaller houses, landings, halls and bays in morning rooms had glass casements strategically placed to provide the effect of luxurious foliage against the light. It was soon found that many of the popular plants, including the famous aspidistras, could thrive happily without proximity to light, and the modern fashion for free-standing pot-plants began. Containers for individual plants were needed and an enormous number of jardinières and plant stands appeared in a variety of styles. One of the most popular was the circular wood-framed container lined with metal and with bodywork of cane panels supported on three, curving legs and with a platform below, often gilded or painted in the classical style. Another type was a rectangular, box-top table on a centre column and platform base, the top having a metal-lined 'well' covered by a lift-off panel, thus enabling its alternative use as an occasional table.

THE SMOKING ROOM AND PARLOUR

Smoking became increasingly popular among gentlemen of the upper and middle classes, and their habit engendered new pieces of furniture. Houses had smoking rooms or 'smoking towers' set aside as apartments not to be entered by ladies. The tower room was a three-quarter circular room attached to the upper exterior corner of a house, giving it a romantic, castle-like appearance from outside. This kind of architectural feature was by no means confined to larger houses, and many examples can be seen on high street corner buildings in both cities and small provincial towns alike, as well as on country mansions. The smoking room required pipe stands and racks, cigar cabinets and cases, a smokers' compendium and a host of smaller gadgets deemed necessary for correct smoking procedure.

Apart from the exclusion of female company from smoking rooms, the Victorian family became a much closer unit, with great importance attached to enjoying

Below left:
A Victorian walnut folding-top work and games table with scroll legs and white porcelain castors, 1860. (B. D. A. Harris of Thaxted)

Below:
The same table, open to reveal the parquetry inlay for chequer and backgammon boards. (B. D. A. Harris of Thaxted)

together individual hobbies such as flower- and model-making, painting and compiling scrap-books, as well as musical evenings and family parties. Such activities were often pursued in the 'parlour' or morning-room, and it is not surprising, therefore, that the parlour suite, consisting of two armchairs, one of which was larger for the gentleman, a three-seat settee and a set of between four and ten single, armless chairs became popular during the middle of the nineteenth century.

An armless chair, as distinct from a dining chair or formal 'side' chair, had originated in the late eighteenth century, when concerts in the music room or recitals in the library were held in more important households and attended by large groups of people. Although the chairs were similar in size and design to the currently fashionable dining chairs, the backs were often inclined at a greater angle to give added comfort and the seats were well upholstered. During the early years of the Victorian age, the distinction between dining-room and parlour chairs remained apparent, but by the 1860s certainly the less wealthy households had combined the two, and so most dining chairs produced during the remainder of the century were made to be suitable for both purposes.

DINING TABLES

By the end of the 1840s, two distinct styles of table had become favourites in Victorian dining-rooms. The first was the circular 'Loo' table, first popularised during the Regency period for the card game of that name, and the second was the extending dining table, in a form dating from the late eighteenth century. The basic construction of the Loo table, with the top supported by a large centre column on a rectangular, circular or triform platform base, carved feet and castors, remained the same until the 1860s. The only variations were the different patterns of decoration. However, during the 1840s it was running concurrently with a new revival of the mid-eighteenth century support, the deeply curved three-or four-legged base. This rapidly became carved or pierced and was generally made of solid rosewood for the best and, later, walnut for the less expensive examples. Plain oval and shaped top centre tables also became popular at this time, as did the swivel and fold-over top tea and card tables. These were all on the centre column and platform base, or the open curved-leg base, rather than having legs placed at each corner, which had been so fashionable during the Regency period.

The most popular version of the nineteenth-century extending dining table was generally made of mahogany and had either semi-circular or severe D-shaped ends. These were made to pull apart to create space for the additional sections or leaves of the table top which were supported by the exposed underframe. There were two basic types of frame: the hinged criss-cross or concertina type, and the sliding type where a series of grooved rails slotted one into another. Both could be extended to seat twelve or eighteen people or reduced to a table for four. The legs were turned and tapering, often with large bulbous flutes or faceted with eight or ten 'sides'. By the end of the century, the elongation was achieved by turning a crank on the end of a long spirally threaded metal rod. During the last decade of the nineteenth century and first quarter of the twentieth, such tables were often supported on cabriole-style legs, the deeply curved knees carved with a mixture of mid-eighteenth-century motifs and finishing with claw and ball feet.

NEW IDEAS

Living as they did amid the excitement of the Industrial Revolution, it is not surprising that the Victorians were obsessed with the succession of new gadgets and inventions for personal and professional aid and household efficiency and comfort. For every section of society from deep-sea divers and aviators to drinkers, smokers, cooks and bottle-washers, and for the partially and totally invalided, there were aids purporting to guarantee success, assistance or cure. Often these were so elaborate as to be absurd but out of it all came one or two really useful ideas. For example, there was the combination hall stand; and the two-seater 'conversation' settee with a small circular tray-top built in the centre.

The chiffonier, another Regency innovation, became one of the most popular Victorian dining-room or parlour wall pieces. As the century progressed, this was often combined with the well-established pedestal sideboard to make a spacious enclosed cupboard below a variety of elaborate superstructures. Depending on styles, these might well consist of shelves, brackets, small cupboards and large overhanging cornices around one central and sometimes several side mirror panels, framed in walnut, mahogany or rosewood according to the status of the piece and decorated with varying degrees of carving according to its cost.

A mid-Victorian calamander, satinwood, purplewood and ivory marquetry side cabinet by Holland and Sons with marquetry designs after Owen Jones, 1870. (See page 2 for a detail of the side panel.)

A gilt and upholstered conversation settee from the mid-nineteenth century. (Mallett & Son Antiques Ltd / The Bridgeman Art Library)

Chapter Seven

THE BEGINNINGS OF MASS PRODUCTION

MACHINE PRODUCTION

THE FIRST wood-carving machine was produced by T. B. Jordan in 1845. The invention of this remarkable machine, which enabled a single man to produce several pieces of identical carved decoration at the same time, altered the entire pattern of the furniture industry for ever. Now, instead of each craftsman in a workshop being restricted to producing one part at a time, a leg, a back rail, or a stretcher for example, it was possible for the same man, using machines that sawed, planed and carved, to produce many parts in the time it had taken to make one. The catch-phrase for the mechanised Victorian era became 'Maximum production for minimum labour'. Unfortunately, the unbridled novelty and freedom that the machine provided meant that, for a while, some most bizarre designs appeared; indeed, much of the furniture produced between 1851 and 1870 seemed to be trying to prove that with this machine the operator could achieve superiority of technical achievement compared to hand-carving. This situation was further complicated by the Warwick School of Carving and its imitators, who were equally determined to prove the superiority of the hand-operated hammer and chisel. Thus the great age of Victorian over-decoration, even on more modest furniture, had arrived. Oak and walnut were the timbers most used, walnut both in the solid and as veneer. Drawer linings on better quality furniture were made mostly of mahogany, the rest being of any cheaper woods, usually pine and deal. The barley sugar twist turning of the Charles II period became popular, combined with under-cut cups of the William and Mary era, with pendant borders and tapering reeded columns from the later eighteenth century. In this way, three fashionable designs from different periods of the seventeenth and eighteenth centuries were often incorporated in one article. Pierced fret-work in the Chippendale manner reappeared, as did panels of marquetry in the classical style. Fret borders were used as galleries at the back edges of shelves and borders of tables to prevent items slipping off, and below the front edges as pure decoration. Panels of fine fret-work were often backed with coloured silk and used for doors or for decoration to the fronts of harmoniums and pianos. Marquetry decorated the backs of chairs and the fronts of cabinets.

Mechanised production, improved techniques of surface decoration and an apparently inexhaustible imagination regarding the use of all kinds of alternative materials gave furniture manufacturers the means to offer their less-wealthy clients deceptively good copies of the finest examples of contemporary design and construction. Unfortunately, the use of inferior materials gave rise to a rapid

Opposite:
By the end of the Victorian period, English tastes were absorbing styles of décor and furnishings from abroad, as a result of the vast Empire. These foreign styles added to the flourishing English furniture industry, which in return was exporting quality and manufacturing expertise all over the world. (Mallett Gallery/The Bridgeman Art Library.)

Above:
A Victorian walnut three-tier whatnot, the tiers above a panelled cupboard.

Above right:
A William IV mahogany and upholstered patent library open armchair with integral footrest in the manner of Robert Dawes of London.

Right:
A William IV walnut and leather upholstered patent reclining chair, J. Alderman patent, 1835. The degree of rake to the back of this chair is controlled by ratchets under each arm.

dilapidation, and the poor-quality furniture of this kind which has survived to the present day can be easily recognised by its generally shoddy condition. Certainly, one of the reasons that so much upholstered furniture of the mid-to-late Victorian periods is now found to be in a rotting and worm-ridden state is that, in striving for cheapness with good effect, bad and often infected stuffings were used instead of the much more expensive, cleaned and curled horse-hair.

UPHOLSTERED FURNITURE

By 1833, quantities of coiled springs for chairs, settees, sofas and bedding were being produced in Birmingham, and it was from this period that fully sprung seats became popular. During the eighteenth century, the upholsterer took into account the design of the chair or seat he had to cover, using the minimum amount of filling to accentuate the contours of the piece. By the 1840s, the seat frame had become more of a vehicle for the maximum amount of plush upholstery the craftsman could apply, thus giving it the appearance of a marsh-mallow on legs, which, by the 1850s, were themselves hidden by deep fringes. During this latter period it became universally popular to further enhance these huge amounts of springs, stuffing, lining and top cover with deep buttoning, giving a dimpled, but difficult-to-clean surface. The Chesterfield-type settee is among the best examples of this finish. Deep buttoning was a development of an earlier, simpler form of decoration limited to more expensive upholstered furniture.

Before the use of coiled springs, the basic webbing on a seat frame extended over the top of the rails. Following their introduction, the webbing was stretched across the bottom edge of the seat rails to support the spring. It was common practice on better quality pieces to cover the underneath with neatly fitting black or neutral material, known as 'bottom canvassing'. By the mid-1830s, the method of 'finishing' the edges of the top cover round seat rails by 'brass-nailing' had gone out of fashion. (Brass-nailing was the application of large brass dome-headed nails along the edge of the material.) Instead, machine-made braid or 'gimp' was used, being fixed with small nails called gimp-pins. During the eighteenth century, an alternative finishing was space-nailing. In this case, a gimble ribbon was attached by the same large dome-headed brass nails at approximately 2-inch intervals.

CONTEMPORARY PUBLICATIONS

While it was now possible for the manufacturer to produce several identical articles at one time, it was becoming increasingly difficult for the moderately wealthy but more discerning client to acquire custom-made furniture. Furniture could now be bought, ready made, in the high street shop, and many of the current books of designs available were used by their authors as a means of critical comment on contemporary bad taste, as well as to advertise their own wares. There were, by the middle of the nineteenth century, several distinct categories of these publications.

The format of eighteenth-century pattern books, such as Thomas Chippendale's *The Gentleman and the Cabinet-Maker's Director* (1754) (see the illustration on page 69) and George Hepplewhite's *The Cabinet-Maker and Upholsterer's Guide* (1788) was continued, either by practising cabinet-makers or by those having close connections with the trade. During the eighteenth century, it was considered increasingly important for architects to design interior fittings and furniture, and by the end of the century the pattern book was no longer the province of the furniture maker alone. It had become a means of portraying ideas for fashionable designs by talented and aesthetically minded patrons of the arts, writers and others. It is quite clear, for example, that Thomas Hope took inspiration from the architect Henry Holland in his publication *Household Furniture and Interior Decoration* in 1807. So, from this time forward, high-style pattern books existed for use as observation and inspiration for the avant-garde, as well as cabinet-makers' catalogues produced by all the leading manufacturers and retailers as illustrated inventories of their currently available stock. Designs in the pattern books of the more influential designers were closely followed by the manufacturers, and their catalogues were evidence to the buying public of the firm's ability to keep up to date with the latest styles.

In 1833, John C. Loudon published the *Encyclopaedia of Cottage, Farm and Villa Architecture and Furniture* and produced a third form of reference book for the nineteenth-century enthusiast, as well as for the present-day devotee. This work, and subsequent similar books, presented a survey of available furniture and design with enormously detailed and often critical texts accompanying the copious illustrations. It was in this medium that many members of the Arts and Crafts movement found considerable freedom of expression later in the century, in the rapidly growing number of regular publications and journals. These, and of course the catalogues to the many exhibitions, provide yet another invaluable source of information concerning this era of the furniture industry and its background.

To the average citizen, though, browsing through the pages of these catalogues meant little more than a chance to glimpse the sort of furniture he was unlikely ever to possess. However, for him there was another source of supply – the second-hand shops or 'furniture brokers' as they were then known. These shops, which sprang up in large numbers in towns and cities across the country, catered for an increasing section of the community whose economic situation changed frequently, as well as for the genuine antique collectors seeking a bargain. The existence of these shops meant that families could trade their furniture up or down according to their circumstances at any given time.

For the student of Victorian furniture in more general terms, other publications have to be considered. Some of the most useful – and most amusing – sources of information available are the advertisements placed in contemporary magazines or directories. Advertisers were keen to promote a huge range of products, many of which have long ceased to exist. However, because of an increasing amount of research and interest in this period, many of the more important of these publications have been reprinted.

THE STRUCTURE OF THE FURNITURE TRADE

Large workshops under the ownership of a single master craftsman were well established long before Victorian times. So, too, was the system whereby craftsmen of different branches of the trade established a shop or warehouse and thereby undertook to supply their clients with everything connected with house furnishing.

In addition, there was the highly complex structure of craft guilds and fraternities which had formalised trading arrangements between journeymen and merchants since the fourteenth century. Journeymen (or yeomen as they were known in the middle ages) were piece-workers. Their name is derived from the French word *journée*, meaning 'day', and for the most part they owned their own tools and were their own masters while they relied on merchants to commission their work. By the end of the eighteenth century, there was also a large number of 'out-workers' who were unaffiliated to, and thus unprotected by, any specific guild or livery company. So it was not uncommon for larger workshops to commission a number of furniture parts such as chair rails from them. Such people were found in the East End of London and in other major cities, and the price for their work was protected only by an ethical sense of responsibility within the trade on the part of the master craftsman. With the advent of mechanisation, such loyalty to workers became uneconomic, and by the mid-nineteenth century many skilled men were without regular employment. Thus, these 'garret masters', as they were called, could be seen hawking their wares from push-carts piled with a week's produce, desperate to sell in order to acquire more raw materials.

Furniture stores were generally showrooms for goods made elsewhere, often from a variety of sources: iron bedsteads from Birmingham, turned fruitwood chairs from High Wycombe, fine mahogany, walnut and rosewood cabinets from London and Lancaster. Higher in the social scale were the showrooms displaying goods made under the supervision of the proprietors, and at the very top were the shops of great names in the furniture industry. These were the fashion leaders, the publishers of catalogues advertising ready-made or custom-built pieces for the wealthiest families or 'carriage trade', a term descriptive of those patrons affording a coach-house and stable in a city. The firms were often long established, employing the finest craftsmen in the land, their names being an automatic guarantee of the best quality product. Among them Messrs Gillow, Smee, Holland, Crace and Arrowsmith should be mentioned. Many other firms specialised in wholesale trade and still more combined the two, with specific warehouses for wholesale and export display, as well as retail showrooms.

It may be easier to understand the tremendous demand for furniture by referring to the enormous growth in population. In 1500, the population of England was less than five million. By 1800, it had risen to nine million and by 1850 numbers had almost doubled again to nearly eighteen million. It is not surprising, therefore, that in 1851, the year of the Great Exhibition, nearly fifty thousand people were employed in two main branches of the furniture industry – cabinet-making and

A pair of Victorian ebonised parcel gilt and polychrome decorated and mother-of-pearl inlaid papier mâché side chairs attributed to Jennens and Bettridge or McCallum and Hodson of Birmingham.

upholstery. As well as new methods of manufacture, new materials were constantly being tried, either for genuine improvement or for the sake of pure sensationalism. Furniture of glass and coal can be safely placed among the latter, whereas modern techniques in the production of already known materials can be recognised for what they were – a real improvement – and it is among these that papier mâché should rate highly.

PAPIER MÂCHÉ

Although Henry Clay first patented the material in England in 1772, papier mâché did not become universally popular until the Victorian period. Literally translated, *papier mâché* means pulped or 'chewed' paper, and the French product by that name used paper in this state for its manufacture. Clay's method was, however, different. Sheets of paper were placed over a mould, each one well pasted to the next. When dry, the shape thus formed was baked to make it extremely hard. Clay was careful to distinguish between his product and true papier mâché by naming it 'paper ware',

A pair of Regency ebonised parcel gilt and brass pole screens with papier mâché fan-shape screens, decorated with chinoiserie subjects.

A Victorian papier mâché tea tray by Benjamin Walton of Wolverhampton, of shaped barbed form and decorated with an estuary view near Cork.

but by the 1830s, the firm of Jennens and Bettridge apparently decided that the original French name sounded much better, even it if was not a true description of the product, and from then on both the cheaper pulped paper and paper ware have been known as papier mâché.

The popularity of papier mâché from 1835 to 1870 is substantiated by the large variety of articles made in this way still to be found all over the country. From tea trays – sometimes in sets of three or four in graduating sizes topped with a matching, high-sided bread basket – to writing boxes, work-tables, tilt-top tables, chairs and even foot and head boards for bedsteads, no article was left untried for the art of the papier mâché maker.

There were essentially two processes involved before a piece of papier mâché was finished – construction and decoration. The surface of the plain or 'blank' article was found to be most ideal for the application of japanning, or lacquer work, the background of which was usually black, although all the primary colours were occasionally used. In the case of pieces from the larger factories in Birmingham and Wolverhampton, manufacture and decoration were carried out in the same establishment while smaller works, specialising in just decoration, bought in their 'blanks' from other similar-sized workshops.

Earlier examples show the use of gold in dust, leaf or paint form, combined with coloured enamels or paints, as the most important ingredients of the decoration. In 1825, however, the application of paper-thin pieces of pearl-shell, known as 'mother-of-pearl' was introduced by George Souter, who worked for Jennens and Bettridge. The shell was applied to the surface of the lacquer and painted with varnish to the required pattern. An acid solution was then applied and the unwanted portions of the shell, unprotected by the varnish, were eaten away leaving the effect of a delightful and deeply translucent insertion to the surface.

Because the basic shapes of papier mâché pieces remained much the same until the late 1870s, the various methods of decoration are frequently the best guide to the approximate date of origin. As a generalisation, the more varied the materials and ingredients applied to and incorporated in the surface, the later the piece is likely to be. The earlier pieces often bore excessive amounts of decoration, but the execution was rarely anything but the very finest quality. The same cannot be said of later papier mâché, which entered a definite decline during the 1870s following massive export orders, saturation of the home market, and an increasing demand for genuine Chinese and Japanese goods at this period. Following the popularity of floral painting, one further important stage in the decoration of papier mâché occurred in 1864, when a patent for the application of powdered aluminium was obtained by Jennens and Bettridge. This gave an added wispiness to the views of romantic historical scenery so popular at this time, but heralded disfavour of the medium.

Another branch of the papier mâché industry was the production of ceiling and wall enrichments and pictures and mirror frames by a method known as 'carton pierre'. This was a French process much improved in England by an important firm of house decorators and furnishers, George Jackson and Sons. The material was pulped paper, mixed with glue and whiting, which was then pressed into moulds and dried in a steady heat. It is still often difficult to distinguish from carved wood. The test is to pierce it with a fine needle. The softer carved wood will permit the insertion of a sharp point; the harder carton pierre will not.

CAST IRON

Cast iron was another unlikely material favoured by the Victorians for the manufacture of certain types of furniture ranging from bedsteads to hall-stands. While wrought iron is hand-forged, cast iron is shaped in moulds and, as the first and last castings from a single mould may be parted by an interval of as much as forty years, dating cast iron can be very difficult. Its impact was profound in many walks of life, affecting the furnishings of cottages and castles. Indeed, the Prince of Wales was so taken with the potential he saw in cast iron (John Nash used it in both the structure and decoration of the Royal Pavilion at Brighton) that he positively encouraged its use at his seaside resort. So popular did it become in the wake of his enthusiasm that soon balconies as well as benches and piers in favourite Royal spas such as Bath, Bristol and Buxton were all adorned with it.

Most nineteenth-century cast-iron furniture came from either French or British foundries, none more famous than the Coalbrookdale foundry at Ironbridge in Shropshire which had been established as early as 1707. By the late nineteenth century, Coalbrookdale was producing a wide range of garden furniture as well as architectural fittings, urns and fountains, many of which are still copied today. The originals were cast to represent some most extraordinary effects including tree roots, trunks and branches as well as complicated vines, ferns and formalised flowers. Many of these patterns date from the mid-1840s and are reflected in other branches of the applied arts, particularly contemporary silverware.

A Victorian oak and bronze gothic revival book carrier, in the manner of A.W.N. Pugin.

The 'Gothic' style, as advocated by A. W. N. Pugin, was also extremely popular for cast-iron furniture. The tracery of Early English and Perpendicular windows, crocketed spires and flying buttresses could be faithfully produced in this medium and have proved popular for present-day copyists. Modern reproductions are usually of aluminium and, while being lighter in weight and rust-proof, are often easily recognisable from the original through the lack of finish at the edges of the mould joints.

A coat, hat and umbrella stand flanked by two garden or hall chairs, produced in cast iron by Coalbrookdale. (The Fine Art Society/ The Bridgeman Art Library)

Chapter Eight

THE ARTS AND CRAFTS MOVEMENT

The heavy, masculine style of furniture that had dominated the drawing rooms of English society during the reign of William IV and the early part of Victoria's reign, with its bastardised 'Etruscan' form, had finally been replaced by the more feminine Old French style first seen during the 1820s. During the 1840s, the Gothic designs of A. W. N. Pugin became another mainstay. Like the Old French, it underwent several adaptations incorporating different materials around the basic theme. A popular example appeared during the 1860s with the use of ebonised wood, usually beech, lightened by low-relief carving decorated with gold.

Mechanisation of the industry provoked a back-lash, and it came with the Arts and Crafts Movement which, from the 1860s, gathered pace through the last half of the nineteenth century and strove to revitalise interest in handicrafts and the applied arts, which seemed under threat from the new technology. The movement really came together in 1861, when the English designer William Morris, unable to find satisfactory furnishings for his new house, founded with some friends the firm of Morris, Marshall, Faulkner & Co. Morris argued that the true basis of art lay in the crafts, and his firm promoted hand-made textiles, wallpaper, furniture and books. Around him gathered a circle of talented artists, architects and others, notably the architects Philip Webb and C. F. A. Voysey (known for his 'cottage' style) the cabinet-maker Ernest Gimson, the ceramic artist William De Morgan and the designers Walter Crane and C. R. Ashbee. The Arts and Crafts Exhibition Society, which was founded in 1888, and the magazines *The Studio* and *Hobby Horse* carried on the traditions of Thomas Hope's *Household Furniture and Interior Decoration* and provided platforms for discussion of the movement's ideas.

THE WARWICK SCHOOL OF CARVING

By the 1860s, the ancient town of Warwick had established itself as one of the important provincial sources of fine furniture with ornate carved decoration. The patterns were so elaborate as to be easily distinguishable from those of similar type produced in other areas, notably London and Newcastle, and were thus recognised and catalogued as being 'Warwick School'. Large sideboards, buffets, cupboards, overmantle mirror frames and other heavy wall pieces were enriched with the most lavish recreations of romantic episodes from the age of chivalry depicted within borders of combined baroque, rococo and classical motifs. The one immediately recognisable feature peculiar to the carving of this period is the lack of sensitivity to proportion so apparent in previous ages; also it is very often historically inaccurate. As a result the style is unmistakable and its effects further reaching than its leaders could have imagined. By the 1880s there could have been few families

Opposite:
A settle designed by Philip Webb and made by Morris & Co., c. 1880. Webb was Morris's close friend and an influential architect and designer for the firm. He preferred well-made, functional pieces in oak inspired by English traditions. This settle, with its high back to protect from draughts, is decorated with designs reminiscent of Morris's textile patterns. (The Fine Art Society/ The Bridgeman Art Library)

whose children were not taught the rudiments of wood carving at classes often run by amateurs. The results were terrible: for the last forty years of the nineteenth century and more, countless numbers of good early (sixteenth- to eighteenth-century) pieces of furniture were 'improved' by shallow carved decoration. For the most part, little importance or veneration was accorded to furniture simply because it was old: rather it was an expendable means of supplying objects to enthusiasts for 'improvement'. The danger is that over a hundred years later, such pieces are often sold as old and important.

WILLIAM MORRIS

As early as 1861, William Morris had already gained the reputation of a strict medievalist with strong beliefs in the eventual self-destruction of good taste and craftsmanship in the furniture trade through over-use of machinery and mass production. The trouble was that neither Morris nor his followers were prepared to see or consider the positive advantages that machinery could offer to the industry. Rather, they insisted that 'modern' furniture needed none of the elaborate decoration currently being applied to it, and taught that more care and time should be taken over faultless construction with each joint being so precisely cut as to negate the need for glue. Unfortunately, it had become evident by the 1860s that machine production was cheaper than individual manual production and that time was the costliest factor in the expanding industry. The majority of the early furniture made to the directions of the Morris movement proved too plain to attract the attention of the wealthiest furniture buyers and was too expensive for the average family.

Furniture by Morris and Co., 1860s and 1870s
The furniture and interiors produced by William Morris's firm became fashionable because of their design quality and workmanship. This setting includes one-off pieces like the St George's cabinet, designed by Philip Webb and painted by Morris, on the far right, and examples of rush-seated Sussex chairs that were very affordable and made in large quantities.

Nevertheless, by 1865, Morris's firm, now known as Morris & Co., had stimulated interest in their type of medieval production. They called the style Modern English Gothic or Early English, intending the name to convey an image of purity and simplicity, its construction relying on pegged joints with the surfaces unpolished. This 'look' was strongly favoured by Charles Lock Eastlake in his publication *Hints on Household Taste*, which appeared in 1868, and much credit should go to Morris's chief furniture designer, the architect Philip Webb, as the prime mover in the manufacture of pieces to the patterns favoured by Morris and popularised by Eastlake.

In 1860, Richard Charles produced the *Cabinet-Makers' Monthly Journal of Design*, a publication that strongly favoured the Early English style, and in 1867 Bruce Talbert, a Glasgow trained architect and designer, published *Gothic Forms Applied to Furniture*. The next phase in the decoration of the Early English style was largely pioneered by the architect William Burges. During the 1860s, Burges was working on the reconstruction of Cardiff Castle for the Marquess of Bute and his designs for the interiors included painted furniture. While the furniture designed by Burges cannot be said to have greatly influenced the furniture industry in general, there must be considerable connection between his fondness for painted surfaces and the much admired medieval-style pieces decorated by the artist Edward Burne-Jones, an example of which was shown at the International Exhibition in London in 1862.

A pair of late-Victorian ebonised William Morris Sussex open armchairs with rush seats, 1890.

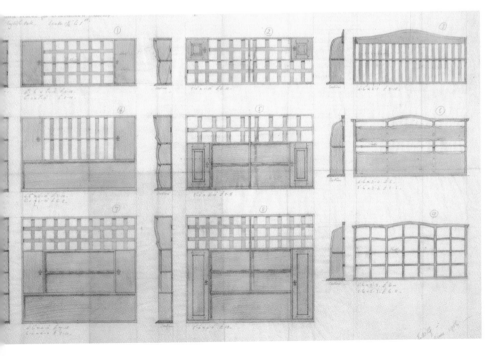

Designs for China racks, sideboards and dressers in oak, 1906, by William Ernest Gimson (1864–1919). (Cheltenham Art Gallery and Museum/The Bridgeman Art Library)

ORIGINS OF ART NOUVEAU

Clearly, the roots of Art Nouveau lay in the styles created by the Arts and Crafts Movement. 'Art Nouveau' was not a term used to describe a particular style until the turn of the century, but the combination of many of the essential ingredients so popular after 1880 was there in the 1860s. However, it was at this time that Charles Eastlake referred to such furniture as 'Art' furniture, striking a distinction between mass-produced and individually crafted pieces. During the final thirty years of the nineteenth century the word 'Art' is seen with increasing regularity in newspapers and journals as a prefix not only to furniture but also to wallpaper and decoration, to such an extent that any new product, even from the cheapest manufacturers, was given this title to secure attention in an increasingly competitive market. But, instead of killing the sale of all art designs, as happened with the over-production and over-sell of papier mâché, enthusiasm for the style increased to such an extent that the development of Art Nouveau from hand-crafted to mass-produced was well under way by the beginning of the twentieth century. At around this time, Monsieur S. Bing opened a store in Paris, selling mainly Japanese goods, which he called *L'Art Nouveau*, and it is from this emporium that the term which was to name a style spanning an era from the 1890s to the 1910s appears to have been derived.

WALLPAPER

Wallpaper was not a Victorian invention. The oldest block-printed wallpaper known in England covers the beams of the dining-room, entrance hall and ceiling of Christ's College, Cambridge, and dates from the early sixteenth century. The design is similar to that of contemporary brocades, but it was not until the late seventeenth century that a repeating pattern was introduced. Scenic panels on wallpapers appeared during the eighteenth century and flock wallpapers, which were first recorded in the 1620s, also became popular. All the major European developments in this industry seem to have taken place in France, but 'European' is specified because of the import and inevitable influence of Chinese wallpaper. Chinese wallpaper had first appeared through the various East Indian companies formed by the major countries in the West during the late sixteenth and early seventeenth centuries: it was given by grateful merchants (Hongs) to important customers. But the delicately painted scenes of exotic birds and flowers quickly created great demand, and a thriving industry in hand-painted rolls of wall-covering grew rapidly. As the concept of western chinoiserie changed during its second great period in the mid-eighteenth century, so too did the essential designs of Chinese wallpaper, and the earlier formal landscapes were filled with figures, birds and animals during the 1750s.

From the mid-nineteenth century, machine printing had an enormous impact on the availability and the price of wallpaper, and at the same time a new, visible link was made between designs for all household fittings and decorations, including wallpaper. It is possible to trace the origins of this link to the creators of the Gothic, Medieval and Early English revival movements in general, with considerable influence from the designs of A. W. N. Pugin and William Morris. The geometric Gothic designs of Pugin's wallpaper in 1843 perfectly complemented his accompanying themes for furniture and fitments, as can be seen from his designs for the Houses of Parliament; and the sinuous, formalised foliate patterns of William Morris, first shown by him for wallpaper in the 'Daisy' patterns of 1862, were repeated on borders, mouldings and cornices, as well as in the shapes of metal mounts on furniture made to his designs. Morris went on to produce a series of wallpaper designs including the now famous 'Pomegranate', 'Trellis' and 'Acanthus' patterns, following which wallpaper gained great popularity among designers as a viable commercial medium for their ideas.

The art of wallpaper design was to become an integral part of the Arts and Crafts Movement and a most important aspect of Art Nouveau. Charles Francis Annesley Voysey, the British architect and designer and one of the most important members of the Arts and Crafts Movement, set up his first important commission for The Cottage at Bishops Itchington in Warwickshire in 1888. In the meantime, he had achieved considerable success with his wallpaper designs for Jeffrey & Co. and had joined the Art Workers' Guild in 1884, exhibiting wallpapers and fabrics at the first exhibition of the Arts and Crafts Exhibition Society and also in 1888 at the time of his work at The Cottage. Voysey was hailed as a 'genius of pattern', and went on to produce his fresh, unassuming designs for wallpapers, textiles and tiles for the rest of his working life.

'Pimpernell', a William Morris wallpaper design from 1876. (The Stapleton Collection / The Bridgeman Art Library)

Glasgow-born architect and interior designer Charles Rennie Mackintosh was also a prime mover in this field. He, too, rejected over-decorated Victorian styles in favour of bare simplicity. He used strong, angular shapes and examples of his work can be seen in most major museums. It is important for any budding collector to view these carefully, for much of his work, being basically simple in structure and design, lent itself to being emulated by other contemporary designers.

Eventually, the artistic approach to design was superseded by commercialism for all but the most wealthy homes, and by 1900 much of what was produced showed little thought or taste in its production. Again, as a result of the revolt against Victorian fuss, there followed a rapid decline in the demand for wallpaper in the early twentieth century. Instead, walls were subjected to a variety of paint treatments in stone or putty colour, relieved only by the panelled effect created by picture rails and door frames.

Chapter Nine

REVIVAL OF OLD STYLES

INTERNATIONAL EXHIBITIONS

Following the success of the Great Exhibition in 1851, further international exhibitions were inevitable. Some alternated between Paris (1855, 1867, 1878), and London (1862, 1871). Vienna hosted an exhibition in 1873, and one was held in Philadelphia in 1876. Australia joined in with shows in both Sydney and Melbourne in 1879 and 1880 respectively. The Eiffel Tower was built for the exhibition in Paris in 1889, and a further exhibition was held in Paris in 1900. This followed the largest previous trade fair, in Chicago in 1893, and broke all records for attendance in the nineteenth century. A Franco-British exhibition was held in London in 1908 and the last before the First World War took place in Brussels in 1910. During the last fifteen years of the century, several newly formed guilds and societies favouring the ideals of William Morris joined forces to create the Arts and Crafts Exhibition Society, which held the first of its three annual exhibitions in 1888. After a short break another exhibition was held in 1893, followed by two more in 1896 and 1899. This, then, was the situation for a fashionable minority group with enthusiasm for artistic and creative craftsmanship within a machine-led environment. A minority it might have been, but its influence was wider and longer lasting than could have been imagined at the time.

REFASHIONING OLD FURNITURE

With the sudden popularity of the exhibitions, there was enormous pressure on the furniture manufacturers to provide new and innovative designs, many of the more elaborate intended for display rather than for practical use. Even so, the majority of what may be considered typical Victorian furniture was made to a high standard and with some semblance of order in its decoration. But the cabinet-makers, working to current designs with new materials, were not the only source of supply. Following the interest in antique furniture, many such craftsmen were commissioned to refashion old pieces, and in this respect the last thirty-five years of the nineteenth century can be seen as the great age of the furniture pastiche.

The carved and turned supports for buffets, the deeply carved uprights and cross-members of panelled furniture, bedposts, complete or in sections, cornice rails and other mouldings were the most popular parts of early oak furniture to be used to create pieces of furniture suitable for smaller but fashionable houses, as well as to furnish the newly built baronial halls of the nouveaux riches.

It is not hard to spot furniture that has undergone such revamping. The frequent inclusion of leaded, glazed door panels (sometimes with stained glass), later carving and new timber are often sufficiently obvious factors to make the piece easily identifiable as Victorian rather than original and of the sixteenth or seventeenth century. Of these three major pointers to watch for, new timber is the least reliable. When such alterations were complete, the whole article was either stripped and polished to a light, honey colour or heavily stained to a dark brown; the wear to edges and borders, which for the first twenty or so years will show a bright colour, has, by the beginning of the twenty-first century, received enough further exposure and polishing to make the contrast less distinct. If doubt remains as to the authenticity of a piece, then look at the size and proportions. People tend to believe that all Victorian furniture was extravagantly large but there was, in fact, enormous demand for smaller pieces bearing the same amount of decoration as their larger counterparts. The reduction in dimensions, the almost too perfect 'squaring-up' of joints and an excessive amount of carving, especially on small cupboards or buffets, coupled with the features mentioned above, should lead to suspicion of the nineteenth-century adaptation.

PERIOD REVIVALS

At the end of the nineteenth century and the beginning of the twentieth, each of the major period styles of English furniture was reproduced. Following the popularity of oak and the Elizabethan, Gothic and Ecclesiastical styles, the Queen Anne style in an equally modified form and the use of walnut became extremely fashionable. From the very end of the nineteenth century to the 1920s, this taste was joined by a vogue for furniture in the Chippendale style, with mahogany as the necessary timber. From about 1895 through to about 1915, there was a demand for lighter, more delicate furniture, which was provided by pieces in the somewhat misnamed Edwardian Sheraton style. The woods used for this were mostly mahogany and satinwood, with considerable accent on the inlaying of a variety of contrasting coloured woods and other materials, such as ivory, mother-of-pearl, enamels and pewter. In each of these period revivals, the use of modern production methods and materials and questionable proportions are usually sufficient evidence of their out-of-period origin.

An alteration that was made in the name of improvement, and perhaps the most common, was the replacement of original old metal handles with turned wooden knobs on the drawers of the chests, tables, cabinets and commodes. Finely turned wooden knobs or pulls had appeared on fashionable furniture during the last quarter of the eighteenth century, and had remained a popular alternative to metal since that time. These were, however, much more an integral part of the overall design of the piece than the large, bulbous mushroom-shaped knobs that came so much into vogue from the late 1860s. The earlier turned knobs were smaller by comparison, and were fixed with a straight dowel glued into a fractionally undersize hole in the drawer front. Victorian knobs were attached by means of a screw-turned dowel fitting into a threaded hole in the drawer front, sometimes without glue, and sometimes going right through the drawer front with a securing nut on the inside.

Sofas like this one gave an air of comfort to middle-class drawing rooms. Spiral spring upholstery was patented in 1826 and the new deeper stuffing was emphasised by buttoning. The show wood frame will usually indicate but not dictate the quality, with rosewood generally being the best and most expensive, then mahogany, then walnut.

A complicating factor during the late nineteenth century was the change in the reasons behind the alterations of authentic early pieces. There are many examples of walnut furniture dating from the eighteenth century which were altered in order to conform with the appearance of the most up-to-date Victorian 'Queen Anne' walnut reproductions. The alterations might have been structural or just cosmetic, involving either considerable cabinet work to reduce size, or merely the removal of all old colour and patina to be repolished with layers of glossy varnish and a new set of handles applied. However, by the time Chippendale-style furniture had once more become fashionable, considerable interest and demand for the genuine article had developed, and the more ordinary household items of the mid-to-late eighteenth century were no longer altered for innocent utility reasons. Instead, they were recarved and otherwise refined for monetary gain. An interest in antiques had arrived and with it came the fakers.

Of the three revived styles that became so popular during the late Victorian and Edwardian period, those of the Queen Anne walnut and Chippendale mahogany furniture were faked to a far greater extent than the Sheraton style. Although a considerable amount of plain furniture dating from the last quarter of the eighteenth century was repolished and re-inlaid in the Sheraton manner, most of this was done as a legitimate 'improvement', simply because little value was attached to the antique or historic interest of such furniture at this time. Nearly all Victorian and Edwardian period repolishing is easily detectable by the hard glossy surface, aptly described by the trade term 'piano polish', over a distinctly stained surface – generally bright ginger for walnut and deep red for mahogany. However, cheaper timber was used for much of the plain provincial furniture of the late eighteenth century, and so the repolisher had to use greater quantities of pre-polish grain filler to prepare the surface of this open-textured wood. When the original old patina, consisting of a primary layer of oil or spirit varnish, followed by many years of waxing and dusting, is removed, the raw surface of the wood is exposed. The more open the grain, the more air penetrates the wood. Thus, when the surface is again sealed with a hard polish, it is only a matter of time before minute air bubbles appear, further drying and shrinking the grain filler to give the effect of pale streaks, where in the original dark lines denote the grain.

BERLIN EMBROIDERY

Pole screens with contemporary needlework, which performed the essential function of screening the fierce heat of the fire from the over made-up faces of the gentry, were particularly popular during the eighteenth century. They also offered an attractive way of displaying decorative panels, either brought from abroad at great expense or produced by the talented ladies of the household. Needlework continued to grow as a popular and rewarding pastime for all classes during the eighteenth century, considerably encouraged by the publication of patterns in the 1730s, usually of floral displays. By the early nineteenth century, patterns were available in a huge variety of subjects, imported from Berlin. The basic principle of the Berlin panel is that of squared paper printed with a pattern in colours, each square representing a stitch of the needlework – similar to the basic principle of painting by numbers.

The first patterns were published in 1793, and the earliest records of their appearance in England are in 1805. To begin with, the cross or tent stitch was used and the wool, which came from Gotha before being dyed in Berlin, was imported with the patterns. However, Wilks of Regent Street, London recognised the potential of this merchandise and by 1831 they were retailing all the imported and home-produced materials and accessories for this embroidery. By 1840, there were some 14,000 different Berlin patterns available. It is from the contrasting colours and complexity of the stitches that nineteenth-century needlework can be approximately dated, the earliest being the most subdued and uniform. Some of the finest examples of the William IV period were executed with silk instead of wool. Cream and white were the most popular colours during the 1830s and 1840s. During the 1850s, black was considered a more suitable background for the violent primary colours that were then fashionable. Unfortunately, fast dyes were rarely used, and much of the original startling effect has been lost through fading. By the end of the 1850s, beads were also incorporated, and the deep pile effect of velvet was obtained by the use of chenille and by making the stitches with long loops prior to cutting in low-relief shapes. From the middle of the century, the most popular designs were floral and ranged from single specimens to enormous intricate displays. By this time, the designs were printed directly on to the fabric. As mass printing was an essential part of the production of the Berlin patterns, it is not surprising that the vogue was subject to considerable criticism from the founders and followers of the Arts and Crafts movement. Such criticism increased towards the end of the century to such a degree that it had a beneficial effect on the rising standard of originality and the quality in both amateur and professional embroidery before general interest and demand declined in the early twentieth century.

A Victorian rosewood Tunbridge ware tea caddy, the top with floral decoration and the sides similarly banded, 1860. Accurate dating of Tunbridge ware can be difficult as it was produced in much the same way following the advent of machine cutting veneer.

TUNBRIDGE WARE

Another decorative medium which faithfully reflected the changing phases in Victorian taste is the veneer known as Tunbridge ware. Originated in Tunbridge Wells, the work looks like mosaic, miniature parquetry or even fine needlework, although its construction is quite different to all three. Long, faceted strips of contrasting coloured woods are glued and bound together until set in a single column. Great skill is needed in the arrangement of these thin strips, for it is during this part of the operation that the desired picture is built up. When the column is dry, slices are cut from the end in the manner of veneer, and these can then be applied to the surface of the article to be decorated.

The earliest records of Tunbridge ware refer to wood turners in that district during the late sixteenth and early seventeenth centuries, and offer evidence that this was a popular method of making decorative turned wood bowls, cups and other small objects. The natural waters in the Tunbridge area were found to have a chemical reaction on some woods, in particular the local oak, which turned a curious green. During the late seventeenth century, when various dyes and acids were often used to change the natural colours of woods, Tunbridge ware became much in demand, and by the end of the eighteenth century all manner of small boxes had lids and sides decorated with panels of geometric or floral patterns. In 1787, one correspondent wrote that, in his opinion, trade in Tunbridge ware would have improved had it first been exported and then introduced as a new 'foreign' merchandise, illustrating once again that the emphasis of demand was on novelty rather than quality. In the nineteenth century, landscapes and fanciful

castles, as well as realistic scenes of local importance, were produced in large numbers on souvenir wares to supply the growing fashion for collecting mementoes of visits, which was to become so important in Victorian life. The development of fine cutting machinery benefited the manufacturers of Tunbridge ware, and its production and popularity reached a zenith during the second half of the nineteenth century.

The hobby of collecting souvenirs first had an effect on furniture in the 1860s. About this time, extra shelf space started to appear in any suitable cabinets, sideboards, dressers and other wall and chimney furniture. The sides of mirror frames were formed of tiers of small shelves, each supported on turned columns and often with pierced galleries around the lower edges and canopies at the top. This concept was adapted for over-mantles and sideboard backs, and the inclusion of panes of mirror-glass to reflect the objects on display added to the apparently required sense of clutter. Graduated corner shelves, both hanging and free-standing, also became extremely popular. As with every other change in basic structure, the side and corner shelves in straight or graduating form were made in every currently fashionable style and give a further idea of the vast range of style and quality available to the general public during the last thirty years of the nineteenth century.

BENTWOOD FURNITURE

Some of the most popular chairs produced in Europe during the nineteenth century were the bentwood pieces produced by the Thonet brothers in Vienna from 1849. Constructed from slender beechwood rods and usually with caned seats, they were light, strong, durable and ideal for mass production. The wooden parts of the furniture were shaped in steam presses and finished in a variety of ways of which the most popular were ebonising or graining in simulation of more expensive timbers. The attractive curved shapes afforded considerable comfort and the cane seats made them economical. Messrs Thonet opened a showroom in London and sold vast quantities. Unfortunately, like many Victorian ideas, bentwood eventually became synonymous with cheap mass production and a brilliant concept became a victim of its own success. However, the production of bentwood furniture, particularly single chairs, continued well into the twentieth century, by which time the traditional cane seat had been superseded by the circular plywood seat, machine-stamped in a variety of shallow relief patterns.

A Victorian bentwood rocking chair by Thonet of Vienna introduced in the mid-nineteenth century and popular into the early twentieth century.

Chapter Ten

ORIENTAL STYLES
AND ART NOUVEAU

T HE ENGLISH FASCINATION with the Orient and its art has lasted for centuries. Certainly after the establishment of the European East India companies in the sixteenth and seventeenth centuries, trade, particularly with China, was brisk. Japan was not such an open market, however, as it remained almost totally cut off from 1664 until the period of the Meiji, or Enlightened Government, which began during the 1860s. During this period of isolation, Japan's limited export of mainly porcelain and some lacquer was carried out from the island of Nagasaki with the Dutch East India Company. The accession of the Emperor Mitsuhito in 1867 led to drastic changes in government policies, and subsequent years saw a gradual lifting of many of the ancient barriers to trade. Despite strong and powerful opposition, Mitsuhito sent his brother to the first International Exhibition in Paris in 1867 to report on the possibilities of trade in a world market. Thereafter, the Japanese government wisely assisted the production of goods that would sell in the West, and in particular found an unexpected and eager demand for her culture and products in England. 'Japanese' was a style that immediately captured the imaginations of aesthetes, historians, followers of the Arts and Crafts movement and a complete cross-section of the general public. Examples of the style were first shown publicly at the second Great Exhibition in London in 1862, and by 1870 the Japanese taste had become a craze that was to affect design in one form or another for the next forty years. Among the chief exponents of the early style were Burges, Godwin, Dresser, Whistler, Leach and the delightfully named Lafcadio Hearn, who probably exercised the greatest and most informed influence of all.

Born on the Greek island of Levkas and brought up in England and France, Hearn emigrated to the USA at the age of nineteen. He worked there as a journalist, until in 1894 a magazine commissioned him to write a series of articles on Japan. Once there, this colourful character could not tear himself away. He described the feudal system of the country in *Glimpses of Unfamiliar Japan* published in 1894. The following year he took up Japanese citizenship, assuming the name Yakumo Koizumi, and became Professor of English Literature at the University of Tokyo. He wrote twelve books about Japan and it was these successful writings which caught the imagination of the British public in general and designers in particular. Authentic and pseudo Japanese goods were first sold in London by Messrs Farmer and Rogers and by Liberty. The style had a tranquil quality, a simplicity of form and an inherent beauty which conveyed something of the timeless Japanese culture, conjuring up pictures of a far-off Utopia brought within reach of every front room and parlour in England. It was during this time that the masses of fans, sun-shades, scrolls and screens, lacquer boxes, ivory carvings, exotic gowns and small items of

Opposite:
Anglo–Japanese style furniture designs by Edward William Godwin (1833–86), c. 1860. Godwin was one of the first designers to introduce the Japanese style to Europe after Japan was opened to the West in 1853, and his influence can also be detected in the furniture of the Arts and Crafts Movement. (The Stapleton Collection / The Bridgeman Art Library)

furniture first started to spread through the home market. The coats, shawls, kimonos and other embroidered silks were machine-made but of sufficiently exquisite quality to lead to the belief that they were of a much earlier date and hand-made.

The already well-organised commercial import of Japanese wares was further supplemented by the individual tourist visiting the Orient. From the large amounts of such merchandise still resting in English homes, it can be assumed that every passenger and crew member of the ships that called at Japanese ports brought home a souvenir. Because the Japanese were so adept at producing their traditional patterns with the help of modern machinery, the tourist had the added incentive to buy in the hope that his purchases might be of antique as well as decorative value, for it was difficult for him to know one from the other. As a result, it is always wise to consult an expert before parting with a 'Japanese' family heirloom, or indeed paying large sums of money for such pieces, although they are now antiques in their own right being at least a hundred years old – machine-made or not!

Bamboo furniture is the most popular type of Japanese furniture still in existence. The asymmetrical designs often incorporated one or several panels of lacquer, with shelves formed of woven rattan cane, sometimes covered with embossed leather.

A re-creation in the Geffrye Museum, London, of a drawing room dating from around 1910. There is a mixture of styles, from the Arts and Crafts fireplace to the Queen Anne revival chair on the left, covered with an Arts and Crafts fabric. (The Geffrye Museum)

It was not long before English manufacturers started to use natural and simulated cane as a decorative feature, and by the 1890s cheap copies of originals were widely available. Inevitably, and just as with previous crazes, over-production simply served to kill off demand. By 1900, Japanese furniture was beginning to lose its place as a fashion leader, but the accompanying decorative objects remained as a standard part of design in varying degrees for many years.

ART NOUVEAU

It will be recalled that the name Art Nouveau came from the Paris shop of S. Bing, whose first dealings were in imported Japanese ware. When Arthur Lasenby Liberty, formerly manager of Messrs Farmer and Rogers, who had dealt so successfully with the Japanese merchandise on exhibition in 1862, opened his now world-famous shop in 1875, the Japanese-style ornaments he sold were known in some quarters as 'Style Liberty'. It was a name that originated in Italy which, at that time, tended to import rather than contribute to the creation of Art Nouveau.

Art Nouveau relied heavily upon the influence of all that had gone before, but with a difference. The heavy Gothicism of William Morris was lightened, the abandonment of Aubrey Beardsley was controlled and even the stark, vertical lines

A Victorian Liberty and Co. birch settee designed by Leonard Wyburd in a Moorish style, the upholstered seat and padded back set within a frame of elaborately pierced Musharabiyeh work. The retailer's label is for Liberty and Co. London, 1888.

of Christopher Dresser, E. W. Godwin and Arthur Mackmurdo were eased in an attempt to appeal to a wider market for the mass-produced furniture industry. Strangely enough, it was the bleakness of the unbending vertical lines so strongly advocated by these men, again considerably influenced by Japanese architecture, which remained into the twentieth century to form the basis for the clear-cut designs of the 'functional' style.

However, most furniture manufactured during the first decade of the twentieth century was to earlier period patterns. The growing interest in genuine antiques continued to influence the faker and improver, and the supply of bogus as well as cheap imitation antique furniture was plentiful. Fully upholstered three-piece suites became popular 'front room' items, and the market was further bolstered by the import of Continental and American furniture. Typical examples of the latter include Japanese-style 'rattan' pieces and the rectangular box-frame chiming clocks with coloured glass panels to the doors.

AMBROSE HEAL

There was clearly a need for a middle range of furniture, of good-quality pieces that could bridge the gap between the expensive exhibition class and the cheaper, mass-produced variety. A pioneer of such furniture was Ambrose Heal who, as a trained cabinet-maker and member of a well-established family business in London,

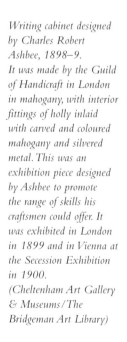

Writing cabinet designed by Charles Robert Ashbee, 1898–9.
It was made by the Guild of Handicraft in London in mahogany, with interior fittings of holly inlaid with carved and coloured mahogany and silvered metal. This was an exhibition piece designed by Ashbee to promote the range of skills his craftsmen could offer. It was exhibited in London in 1899 and in Vienna at the Secession Exhibition in 1900.
(Cheltenham Art Gallery & Museums / The Bridgeman Art Library)

showed considerable foresight in his designs for bedroom and, later, general household items. The characteristics of his furniture were plain, symmetrical lines showing much influence of the later Art Nouveau and Japanese styles, with unpolished or 'weathered' Japanese oak, sometimes 'limed', as the most used timber. Japanese oak was used in preference to the European variety as it was found to have a much closer grain and possess central rays of much stronger, contrasting colour. The designs were produced with commercial manufacture in mind and, by the early 1900s, his success in filling such an obvious hole in the market became apparent. Within a very short time, many of Heal's ideas were accepted as standard patterns for contemporary manufacture in a range of qualities. The more important and exhibition pieces were often decorated with inlay in traditional English manner, and chequered bands of various materials were a popular motif. The more ordinary pieces were essentially plain, any decoration taking the form of a moulded edge to drawer fronts in a simplified mid-sixteenth-century style, or geometric patterns created by the juxtaposition of timber grain – for example, the very popular circle within a quartered square door panel. Drawer and door handles were of turned wood or sunken, the drawer front being pierced in an elongated oval or heart shape with sufficient undercut at the top for the fingers to secure a grip. Kitchen furniture – tables, rush-seated chairs, cupboards and dressers – had the appearance of extremely elementary construction, but the high quality was, and still is, easily discernible through the choice and treatment of the timber and the precision with which the joints were cut.

Demand for symmetrically designed furniture with increasing severity in its functional appearance grew steadily through the 1920s and 1930s, equalling and gradually overtaking the popularity of the period and Eastern styles.

A Heal's writing table in limed oak, c. 1920. This piece was developed from a table designed by Ambrose Heal with the architect, Philip Tilden, and made for Winston Churchill by Heal's cabinetmakers. Heal promoted the use of weathered and limed oak after 1918 to appeal to a market that wanted easy-to-clean surface finishes. (Christie's Images / The Bridgeman Art Library)

Chapter Eleven

FAKES, ALTERATIONS AND IMPROVEMENTS

T HE COMPLETE FAKE is an article made with old materials, in the old method of construction, by a highly skilled craftsman and for the sole purpose of deception. Such pieces have been made for well over a hundred years and early examples can be quite difficult to spot, having had three or four generations of genuine wear and tear. Unfortunately, there is no quick way to detect them. It is instinct and a trained eye that will notice something wrong and experience that will identify the faults.

A fake will usually have some fault, most often in its proportions, which shines forth like a guilty secret. 'It stands wrong' is a highly descriptive trade expression which assesses and dismisses in one, and this is sufficient if more interest need not be shown. But when large amounts of money are involved, as is often the case, close attention must be given and cogent reasons found and supplied. At this stage, the piece is subjected to detailed investigation of timber joints, glue, screws, nails and pegs. Is there dust and dirt where there should be none or vice-versa? The same goes for any piece which is not genuine, whether it be old but subsequently altered, later enhanced with carving, made up entirely from several old pieces, part of a genuine piece 'married,' or suspect for any other reason, however innocent that reason might have been. Arriving at a definitive conclusion can be extremely testing, but here are a few guidelines. To begin with, try to memorise a series of points that can quickly be brought to mind.

Firstly: consider the shape, the use and the material to give the earliest possible date.

Next: scrutinise the colour and surface condition, the patina and signs of wear.

Then: examine the construction, wood behaviour and unexposed wood condition.

Shape, use and material should all be compatible and will signify the earliest date an article could have been made. For example, given a mahogany dumb-waiter with column supports and swept tripod base in the classical style, think to yourself if it is in mahogany – then it must be after 1725; the dumbwaiter appeared after 1745; a dumb-waiter in the classical style must be after 1775, therefore the earliest possible date is 1775.

Having established the date, look for colour and surface condition. For example, supposing you want to date an oak sofa table on a centre column support, remember that oak means it could be Elizabethan, that is some time between 1558 and 1601. However, sofa tables were not made before 1780 and sofa tables did not stand on centre columns until after 1800, therefore the earliest possible date for your table is post-1800.

Opposite:
Patina is the word used to describe the desirable surface on antique furniture. The original treatment of the timber when a piece of furniture was finished but unpolished has created different patinas for us today, and so to fully appreciate the subtleties of 'patina' it is important to understand the various methods of polishing that were adopted at different periods over a span of three hundred years.

PATINA

Since craftsmen first took pride in their work, the outer surfaces of furniture have had some sort of preservative treatment when they were new. Following the decline in popularity of painted furniture during the sixteenth century, after application of a grain filler, the use of either an oil polish or a polish of beeswax and turpentine became standard practice. The main difference in the effect of these polishes is that, through oxidisation, the oil polish caused wood to darken whereas the beeswax sealed it and retained the mellow colour. The use of oil or wax polish continued on country furniture until the nineteenth century, but during the early 1660s the use of varnish became most popular on all fine furniture, particularly that decorated with veneer. The first type of varnish used in the seventeenth century was made with oil and resin. Thin coats of this mixture were applied to the surface of the wood, allowing time between each coat for the resin to dry out the oil. During this process, the hardened surface was rubbed with one of a variety of mild abrasives, which eventually filled the grain and left the timber well protected, of good colour, and ready for its first beeswaxing. Oil varnish was superseded during the 1670s by spirit varnish. This consisted of spirits of wine and gum-lac and was known as China varnish, introduced to England from the East where it was used to preserve the fine lacquer work imported into England at that time. As with the lacquer work itself, the materials were not available in western Europe to make China varnish but before long a suitable alternative had been discovered. This was basically the same formula with a spirit base but either seed-lac or shell-lac was used instead of the gum-lac. The method of application was essentially the same as for the oil varnish. During the early 1820s, an easier and inferior method of obtaining an immediate lustrous surface came from France. It was called 'French polishing' and consisted of

A provincial oak settle of plain panelled construction, introduced in the late seventeenth century and popular throughout the eighteenth century. Such pieces would have received either an oil or wax polish on completion.

soaking with shellac and spirit. Several applications of this are made to the surface of the furniture, without the need for rubbing down between each, until a glass-like finish is achieved. French polish is not as durable as oil varnish; it chips and wears away and is easily marked by heat and damp.

Sadly, many pieces of earlier furniture have had the original patina stripped away to be French polished during the nineteenth and twentieth centuries. This detracts considerably from the merit of an article and can often be recognised by close examination of the grain. To prepare a recently stripped and therefore open grained surface for French polishing, the grain has first to be filled. During the nineteenth and early twentieth centuries, ground pea-flower, whiting or plaster of Paris were most often used. These were stained the appropriate colour and when dry the French polish was applied. Over the years the stain has bleached, leaving the grain marked with pale brown or white flecks. This does not occur on the surface of English furniture made before the early nineteenth century, which retains its original finish or patina.

Whatever the colour of an article, it should have a good patination. Patination describes the condition of the surface after years of waxing, the accumulation of grease and dirt and the multitude of small scratches resulting from general but not careless use. During the eighteenth century, the application of oil (as used for polishing a gun-stock), wax and varnish were all used for polishing English furniture. Oiling and waxing were considered most suitable for chairs and smaller articles constructed in solid undecorated mahogany, and varnishing was preferred for most veneered surfaces. Over a long period of time, dirt and wax have not only filled the grain but have built up into small ridges above the surface caused largely by the shrinkage of the timber. These ridges can be seen when viewed obliquely against the light and cannot be reproduced, thus providing a guarantee of at least an old top, leg, rail or stretcher. On veneered surfaces, the varnish filled and sealed the grain, so there is no raised grain effect, but fine ridges caused by the glue pushing through between the lines of stringing and crossbanding can be seen, again when viewed obliquely. So, for the most part, it is the colour, absence of pale grain filler and the other elements of patina mentioned above, which are the guides to the authenticity of surface condition on furniture of the late eighteenth century.

SIGNS OF WEAR AND USE

Whereas the signs of wear in the patina concern the outer surfaces, signs of use relate to the effects of handling and the movements of working parts. Most early oak and walnut furniture made for the downstairs rooms originally stood on a stone floor that was frequently washed with water. Water will gradually rot wood and so one would expect to see signs of the feet having been eaten away and discoloration three or four inches up each leg. However, when the feet became unsteady, it was common practice to cut them off as far as necessary and many early stools and chairs have the bottom rails at floor level as a result. Unfortunately, a great many more have had the feet replaced, often so badly that proper restoration is made more difficult.

Each time a piece of furniture is moved, it has to be lifted up. When you next lift a piece of furniture, note where your fingers touch it. It will have been moved in the same way since it was first made and as a result it will be darker in these areas from the natural oils of hands and the accumulation of dust and dirt. In some instances, a natural patina will have been created. However, the rest of the underside should be dry looking, paler and perhaps dusty but not stained or polished. This applies without exception to chair and stool rails, drawer linings and, in most cases, table frames. Close scrutiny of the movement of working parts where two wood surfaces rub one against another should always reveal corresponding friction marks. The underneath of gate-leg table leaves, where the leg pulls out in an arc to support the leaf, drawers and their runners and hinged doors that have fractionally dropped to rub on the frame or rail are typical examples.

While the faker seems to have ignored the simulation of hand holds underneath furniture, he has certainly spared no effort and imagination in achieving an instant patina on the outer surfaces of show wood. The effects of discoloration of most timbers can be gained by using chemicals. In the past, the country faker achieved the appearance of age and rotted, water-marked feet by standing furniture in a regularly used stable! The acidity therein condensed the work of 200 years into a few months. All manner of implements such as chains, small pieces of clinker as well as conventional tools of the workshop were used to obtain the bruises and scratches that occur with constant use and form an integral part of patina. But here, too, the enthusiastic faker so often gives himself away by overdoing the 'distressing'. This occurs when signs of use appear on places where it would not be expected and closer inspection reveals the distressing to be too regular in pattern.

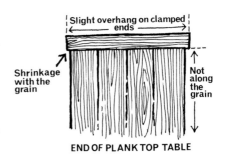

END OF PLANK TOP TABLE

WOOD'S BEHAVIOUR

As wood ages it shrinks and contracts across the grain, not along it. This can provide us with several clues. For a start, willow pegs securing mortice and tenon frames on seventeenth-century stools and chairs should remain protruding fractionally above the outer surface due to shrinkage of the rail. The peg might be fractionally smaller in diameter, but it will be no shorter. This shrinkage element applies to a greater or lesser degree to all timber and is very important factor when viewing country or very early furniture, made at a time and in circumstances when less well seasoned and matured woods were used. It is especially evident on the tops of farmhouse type oak tables where the cleated ends should be a little wider. This is because the top will have shrunk across its width leaving the cleats protruding sometimes as much as a quarter of an inch. It is also worth remembering that on most early mortice and tenon joined frames the original willow pegs were rarely cut off on the inside of the joints. These peg ends are always good to see, but it is not sinister if they are not present.

DECORATION

All types of decoration, from carving, veneering, painting and inlaying, have been executed on earlier and originally plain furniture at some time or another. This might have been done to improve the value or simply and innocently to bring the piece up-to-date. The fact is that such a piece is no longer as it started life and is therefore no longer totally genuine. In most cases it is fairly obvious, although later painted decoration in the classical style, particularly on Sheraton and Adam period pieces, can be a problem. Later carving is perhaps easier to spot. When an eighteenth-century chair maker planned to decorate his chair with carving, he allowed sufficient timber for the motif to stand proud of the outline or the leg or rail. The re-carver or faker had no such opportunity and had therefore to cut into the timber to give the impression of relief. If the carving does not appear raised above the outline of a curved surface, it is unlikely to be contemporary.

VENEERS

Antique furniture from the walnut period, of around 1690–1736, has always commanded a higher price than oak, and many early oak bureaux and chests have been later decorated with walnut veneer for that reason. However, with the exception of clock cases and, occasionally, pieces of the finest quality, as a general rule in English furniture walnut veneer was rarely applied to an oak carcase. Pine and deal were used to make furniture intended to be veneered, with only the drawer linings or other parts that would show being made of oak. In addition, remember that the veneer should be thick, being saw-cut by hand, and thus rarely less than $\frac{1}{16}$-inch thick. Thin, machine-cut veneer was not produced until the nineteenth century, during which the technique developed and by 1900 paper-thin veneers were being produced. It is possible to check the thickness of veneer at an open or unfinished edge, a chipped corner, a crack or slight bubble in the surface (press with fingers to see how easily it yields), or where a piece of stringing has come away. Thin veneer on any seventeenth- or eighteenth-century English furniture is always suspicious and will be the result of either the surface being scraped down – perhaps to remove deep scratches, bruises or stains – or the later application of a more luxurious wood.

While oak had seldom been used as a base for walnut veneer, in the mid-eighteenth century it was much used for mahogany veneer on better-quality furniture. Mahogany, like walnut, was first used in the solid, but by the middle of the eighteenth century the demand for fashionable furniture was so great that it also became used as veneer, mostly onto oak. By the end of the century, when it was more plentiful and less expensive, it was also employed as background for veneers of satinwood, rosewood, kingwood etc. and cedar was often used for the linings of small drawers in the finest quality pieces.

Just as the nineteenth- and twentieth-century re-carver improved originally plain eighteenth-century furniture when the styles of Chippendale and Hepplewhite became so popular, so the inlayer and veneer worker applied his craft to similar pieces during the period of what is now known as Edwardian Sheraton. Whereas the absence of raised carved decoration is a guide to authenticity through the alteration of the surface depth, the later inlayed pieces provides a less obvious give-away. The wood removed to take decoration is replaced with panels of marquetry, stringing and cross-banding and the surface covered with layers of French polish. However, where this has been done, the surface is slightly dented. This is clearly discernible when viewed obliquely against the light.

Oval shells, corner fans, box wood stringing and satinwood cross-banding are among the features most commonly used at this time, and it is through the later craftsman's ignorance of the eighteenth-century original that it is possible to recognise his work, for the motifs were applied in such profusion that their very variety is enough to arouse suspicion.

HANDLES

Early eighteenth-century handles or pulls were of the pendant, back plate and split-pin type. These needed only a small hole in the drawer to take the tag and might have a small dent or pin hole three-quarters of an inch above and below the hole inside the drawer where the tag was fastened. By the 1730s, swan-neck drop handles were secured by two screw-threaded bolts fixed with small nuts inside the drawer. Behind the swan-neck drops there were solid, shaped, back plates which, by the 1750s, became pierced with rococo, Gothic and Chinese designs. By the 1770s, the back plates had gone out of fashion, leaving just the swan-neck drops. They returned in a new form in the late 1780s, when developments to the steam press enabled

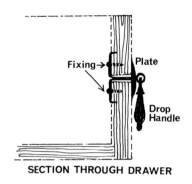

SECTION THROUGH DRAWER

oval and circular plate handles, with elaborate scenes and motifs incorporating the drop handle, to be mass-produced. For smaller pieces, brass knobs and finely turned wooden knobs became popular. During the nineteenth century, it was fashionable to remove any old metal handles and replace them with turned wood knobs. Modern castings of old handles have made it possible to restore the original appearance to a piece of furniture quite easily, and the correct style of handle can be identified from illustrations in eighteenth-century design books.

WOODWORM

Evidence of woodworm is not necessarily a sign of age in furniture. Woodworm belongs to the same species as the death watch beetle, and generally attacks furniture in poorly ventilated conditions. Woodworms eat into timber, leaving small round holes visible on the surface. Then they change direction and rest just below the surface where they go through various phases of development before emerging. They lay their eggs in spring and their greatest activity is during the summer months. Use of a well-known worm killer is the best treatment, but for severe damage an expert should be consulted. Woodworms burrow in and out of timber, never along the surface, so when any part of a piece of furniture has the surface disfigured with semi-circular channels and worm holes, it must have been cut from timber previously used on another piece of furniture. No cabinet-maker would have used ugly timber originally, but in an attempt to add years, a faker just might!

ALTERATIONS

Of all the furniture produced through the centuries, probably the most commonly 'improved' piece is the plain-top, tripod-base tea table. To find out whether the base and top are the same period, tilt the top and look carefully at the areas where the block, the underside of the top and the insides of the runners all meet. As such tables were more often closed than tilted, these areas will have been less exposed to the air and dust and should therefore appear slightly cleaner. Friction marks on the insides of the runners and edges of the block, caused when the table has been opened and closed, should correspond. If the metal latch and ends of the tenons or bird-cage columns protrude slightly above the surface of the block, there should be corresponding bruises on the top made when it closed. Such protrusions will have occurred because the block has shrunk slightly across the grain of the timber.

The fact that the timber shrinks across and not along the grain may be useful. A tray top is 'dished' on a lathe and is perfectly circular when new, but an original eighteenth-century tray top will rarely be so, for the timber will have shrunk slightly. If a tray top is found to be precisely circular, it is likely to have been altered within recent times and needs a closer look. An authentic tray top will have been turned from a thick piece of timber. A top intended to be plain was of thinner timber as there was no need to allow for dishing. Therefore when an originally plain top has been altered to a tray at a later date, the ends of the fixing screws for the runners will have been exposed. These can be easily cut off, but the holes will still be evident and, to camouflage them, the top will have been falsely scratched or bruised at regular intervals. Note the position of the runners under the top and then carefully examine the top surface for two corresponding rows of eight equally spaced marks. The gallery edge supported on small turned pillars found on fine torchères and tripod tables from the 1755–75 period was invariably made in sections to give extra strength, whereas a 'pie-crust' or other raised and shaped edge was carved from the solid.

For more than a hundred years, many two-part pieces of furniture such as tallboys, bureau bookcases and cabinets have been separated and many original single pieces have had upper parts added. This was often done without thought or care for the original, thus providing several points to look for. Two-piece furniture evolved from the cabinet or chest on stand of the late seventeenth century and the method of securing the top to the bottom remained unchanged. Either the top or the lower part of the stand had a retaining moulding fixed on each side and the front to secure the base of the cabinet. This retaining moulding was seldom applied to the cabinet, and the top of the base which was to receive the cabinet was rarely veneered.

When a chest of drawers was made as a dressing chest, the top was intended to be used and visible and therefore decorated with veneer. When the same structure was made as the upper part of a tallboy, the top was too high to be seen, and therefore was not veneered. Many top parts of tallboys have had feet added to make them into fashionable small chests, but the proportions of the large, overhanging moulding at the top edge and the similar moulding at the base, which has to be made to balance, should be enough to arouse suspicion even if the top had been convincingly veneered at the time of its alteration.

It should never be forgotten that domestic English furniture was always intended for use as well as decoration. Treated with care and respect, old furniture can add warm atmosphere and character to a home and most important of all, it will continue to improve in appearance while providing the owner with a pleasing and tangible piece of English history.

Throughout this book, I have attempted to provide a practical guide to a complex subject. Do not be disheartened if some aspects of the furniture you are looking at do not fit with all that you have read. Even people with a lifetime's involvement, whether they be museum curators, auction house cataloguers, collector-connoisseurs or dealers such as myself will tell you gleefully, and without a moment's hesitation, that scarcely a day goes by without something turning up which surprises, confuses and delights us by contradicting those tenets we have come to accept as gospel. That is part of the fascination.

INDEX

Page numbers in italic refer to illustrations